"WAS YOU EVER IN DOVEDALE?"

Derbyshire from Dracula to the Derby Ram

To Sam Totten

– the first

About the author

Edward Garner was born in Derby and after completing his formal education at Derby Central Grammar School joined the staff of the *Derby Evening Telegraph* for three years before enlisting in the Army. That turned into a twenty two-year career commitment and afterwards he went to live in Ireland with his family (his wife, Ann, is a native of Co. Cork). There he remained for the best part of twenty years and gradually took up his old career in journalism, mainly as a freelance. Three books were written as well as numerous articles, some of which, re-written, are contained in *'Was You Ever In Dovedale?'*. A few were broadcast on RTE (Ireland's radio and television network); others were taped by Ann for the library for the blind. In 1989 he returned to Derby and for some years continued to write his bi-monthly column for a Cork newspaper. A decision to give up writing was swiftly followed by a recantation and, eventually, *'Was You Ever In Dovedale?'*.

Also by Edward Garner

Massacre at Rathcormac

To Die by Inches (an account of the Irish Famine)

Curious Tales from North Cork

“WAS YOU EVER IN DOVEDALE?”
Derbyshire from Dracula to the Derby Ram

Edward Garner

Published by Sigma Leisure – an imprint of
Sigma Press, 1 South Oak Lane, Wilmslow, Cheshire SK9 6AR, England.

British Library Cataloguing in Publication Data
A CIP record for this book is available from the British Library.

ISBN: 1-85058-449-4

Typesetting and Design by: Sigma Press, Wilmslow, Cheshire.

Cover photograph: Wolfscote Dale, Derbyshire *(Graham Beech)*

Illustrations: With the exception of those on pages 30, 48, 101 and 110, all the illustrations were drawn by the author.

Cover Design: The Agency, Wilmslow

Printed by: MFP Design & Print

Preface

This book is a portrait of Derbyshire of not just one face but many. There is not a set pattern, such as one of those fascinating local histories, or a description of the county's many interesting buildings. Instead it is a look at such diverse subjects as body-snatchers, strikes, invading armies, not to mention a plot to murder the prime minister.

Sometimes there is a re-telling of well-known Derbyshire topics with an attempt to look at them in a slightly different way or maybe explore the background a little deeper and put the subject more in context.

There are chapters dealing with lesser known aspects of the county, even virtually forgotten ones. Such as witches and an explanation of why they were so feared and persecuted; one of history's minor holocausts. There was a time when a husband could sell his wife by auction and this odd trade is looked at closely with a suggestion as to its origins.

Almost certainly being written about for the first time is the Derby connections with the notorious 19th-century courtesan Lola Montez; she nearly settled down in the town. Not many people are aware that the creator of gruesome 'Sweeny Todd, the Demon Barber of Fleet Street,' made his last stage appearance in Derby; and Dracula made his first.

For those who may notice the title breaks a simple rule of grammar, they are quite right; but since it is a quote from a letter written by Lord Byron to the poet Thomas Moore while living near Ashbourne, then it has to be.

Edward Garner

Acknowledgments

Many people ought to be thanked for their part in the preparation of this book. But they are people whose names I never knew or, sadly, have become forgotten over the years. For it was they who first told me some of the many things encountered in these following pages. Maybe I heard them when out walking the Derbyshire hills and dales as a youngster or at school during lessons in our local history. More than one I first heard when living in Ireland, from people who, learning I was from Derbyshire, told me what they knew. To all of them I give my sincere thanks.

There are others. The staff of Derby's excellent Local Studies Library for their unending patience and expertise. Paul and Gill Robotham for their interest and encouragement, and the latter especially for her knowledge of word processors when rescuing on more than one occasion the script when it threatened to 'byte the dust'. I must remember Bruce Seymore of Piedmont, California, whose extensive research on Lola Montez has been invaluable to me and should for him lead to a successful major biography of an extraordinary woman who so nearly came to settle in Derby.

And not for the first time my sincere thanks to Ann, whose understanding, patience and advice were essential to any success this book might enjoy.

Contents

1. **"Was you ever in Dovedale?"** 1
Not a well-known fact is that the Irish poet, Thomas Moore, composer of world-famous songs, lived near Ashbourne and knew Dovedale well.

2. **Enter the Count** 7
Strange as it may seem, it was a Derby audience that first thrilled to Bram Stoker's Dracula when that Prince of Vampires made his stage debut.

3. **The Resurrection Men** 13
Derbyshire is a long way from where the notorious body-snatchers Burke and Hare operated, but graves were being plundered here, too.

4. **An Old Industry** 19
Huge stone mill-wheels are symbolic of Derbyshire, and their story goes back a great many years.

5. **Trouble at T'mill** 23
Conditions in the old cotton mills were harsh, but one tale about them is both harrowing and rather mysterious.

6. **Where the Tide Turned** 31
When Bonnie Prince Charlie advanced on Derby, the local militia fled; one village, armed with a musket, prepared to fight.

7. **The Princess and the Wolves** 39

A grim tale set in Ilam, with a handsome young man losing his beautiful Irish bride to a pack of wolves.

8. **Unique – Purpose Unknown** 43

One of Derbyshire's most famous buildings, probably unique, and no one knows its original purpose.

9. **When Lola Came to Town** 47

She was Europe's most notorious courtesan who liked Derby and wished to settle – so why did she flee?

10. **And the Walls Came Tumbling Down** 55

Now it is only a memory, but Derby's Manor Hospital was once a workhouse, and home to a talented artist.

11. **A Gin at the Magpie** 61

Once Derbyshire was famous for its lead mines, and the now strange-looking gin was a common sight.

12. **Fall from Grace** 67

Kedlestone Hall's fallen statue and the story of a disgraced poet.

13. **Death of the "Demon Barber"** 69

The man who terrorised Fleet Street and Epping Forest and 'murdered' Maria Marten, died peacefully in Derby.

14. **"And what am I offered?"** 73

If Derbyshire wives in years gone by proved too troublesome, then off to market they went, to be sold by their husbands.

15. Black Jack, Bleu Jaune . . . ? 81

One of the more persistent tales told about Derbyshire's most famous gemstone, and dreamt up by a salesman.

16. "According to Custom" 87

Chesterfield folk decided they did not like one of the more barbaric of military punishments performed in their town.

17. The Gibbet and the Gallows 93

Once executions were public, then a Derbyshire poet decided he had seen enough.

18. A Rabbi Fleet of Foot 99

Ordinarily he was a Heanor jack-of-all-trades, but on the athletics field he was, for a while, unbeatable.

19. Those Curious Ley Lines 103

Just an extraordinary coincidence, or is Arbor Low a collecting point for mysterious lines of prehistoric power?

20. "The Sailors' Friend" 109

Almost forgotten now by Derby people, but once they elected an MP who brought in a world-famous safety measure.

21. "I met the finest ram, Sir" 117

Derby's giant ram, just a figment of some Victorian song writer, or is the beast actually many centuries older?

22. Lock-out **121**

The first major union strike in England took place in Derby, until it was defeated by a 'union' of employers.

23. Man's Best Friend **127**

In one of the worst winters experienced in Derbyshire, a dead man was guarded for over three months by his faithful dog.

24. Conspiracy? **133**

There certainly was a conspiracy, but was it really a Derby family planning to kill the Prime Minister?

25. Witches **143**

Religion unleashed a centuries-long vendetta against witches, and Bakewell witnessed one of the more disgraceful episodes.

26. Nothing More to be Said **149**

A truly remarkable story from the occult realms, and this mass resurrection happened in Hayfield – so it is said.

1

"*Was you ever in Dovedale?*"

The Hanging Bridge at Ashbourne, named to commemorate local belief that some of Bonnie Prince Charlie's ill-fated Jacobite soldiers were so executed there, carries the traveller over the River Dove from Derbyshire into Staffordshire. The river is not named after the bird, as some might think, but is a corruption of the Gaelic word *dubh*, meaning black. Once across, a side road winds up a steep hill to Mayfield and, after a sharp left turn down Slack Lane, there stands high up on a bank a cottage of which its most famous resident wrote to a friend, "You can't think how much our cottage is admired, though 'tis a nutshell of a thing". To another he wrote, "I have got a pretty stone-built cottage in the fields by itself, about a mile and a half from the sweetly situated town of Ashbourne, for which I am to pay £20 a year rent . . . "

Ashbourne's magnificent 13th-century parish church of St. Oswald is an elegant structure and on many an evening the cottage's new resident would listen to the pealing of its bells from high in the graceful spire and hear the echoes as they skipped and chased each other along the valley to "nutshell" Mayfield Cottage. Then one day, so 'tis said, he sat down and immortalised those glorious sounds in a poem, some lines of which recorded:

Those evening bells! Those evening bells
How many a tale their music tells
Of youth, and home, and that sweet time
When last I heard their soothing chime.
And so 'twill be when I am gone;
That tuneful peal will still ring on
While other bards shall walk these dells
And sing your praise, sweet evening bells!

Those lines are not the work of a local versifier but were first recorded in the Irish lyricist Thomas Moore's musical collection, *National Airs*.

Thomas Moore, son of a Dublin grocer, once commented that the Irish never fought or wrote well on their own soil. Of the gentler calling he was a perfect example. Born in 1779 he graduated from Trinity College and after that spent much of his life in England. The longer he did so his gentle patriotism grew in proportion and provided a rich vein of inspiration for his world-famous songs, contained in ten issues of *Irish Melodies.* Of those, the best known must surely be *'Tis The Last Rose of Summer* and *The Minstrel Boy*, both first published while Moore lived at the cottage. The *Irish Melodies* alone kept Moore in a fine income for life of around £500 a year.

The need for peace and quiet brought Moore to Mayfield, essential for him to write *Lalla Rookh*, an exotic Oriental romance for which he would be paid £3,000, an extraordinary sum in those days for a poetic work. Public appetite for such extravagances had been whetted by Byron, friend and confidant of Moore, notably with *The Corsair* published in 1814 and which he dedicated to the diminutive Irishman.

Delighted and hugely flattered by the compliment, Moore assured his many Ashbourne friends that it was nothing for a poor poet to dedicate a poem to a great lord, "but it is something passing strange for a great lord to dedicate his book to a poor poet." After *Lalla Rookh* appeared Byron wrote to the Irish poet, "I suspect you have written a devlish fine composition." Moore completed the poem while still at the cottage but publication problems delayed its public appearance until after his departure. The massive work, running to over four hundred pages, was an instant success that eventually went world-wide. Literary opinion declared that *Lalla Rookh* ranged its composer alongside Byron and Sir Walter Scott.

Byron knew Derbyshire well and in a letter to his friend asked of him, "Was *(sic)* you ever in Dovedale? I can assure there are things in Derbyshire as noble as Greece or Switzerland." For which sentence people of that county have forgiven the profligate lord most things and the tourist board offered up thanks. As for Moore, he considered Dovedale "the very abode of genii." A further communication from Byron told Moore that he would "take a cottage a hundred yards south of your abode, and become your neighbour." Then the poetical pair could spend their days together and "we will compose such canticles and hold such dialogues." Byron never did visit Moore at Ashbourne; in any case the noble lord had gone into voluntary exile in Europe during Moore's last year at the cottage.

Undoubtedly Moore was flattered to have the great man's friendship but sycophancy played no role in his nature. And as for Byron there is no doubt he held the tiny Irishman in high esteem. Exiled in Europe, away from the society he had affronted once too often, Byron maintained a lively correspondence, constantly seeking news.

What are you doing now,
Oh Thomas Moore?
Sighing or suing now,
Rhyming or wooing now
Billing or cooing now,
Which, Thomas Moore?

Thomas Moore came to Mayfield Cottage in 1813, three years

after meeting Lord Byron for the first time. He came as the proud father of a little girl. His wife, an attractive English actress named Bessie Dyke, he had married two years before and as newly-weds they established their first real home near Kegworth in Leicestershire. Moore felt a need to live in the peace of the countryside and also to be near the Donington Hall seat of his patron, Lord Moira. Accounts agree that the marriage proved a most happy and enduring union, although in a time when actresses as a rule were not accepted in the social milieu in which her husband had become a noted celebrity and always made welcome. He was sometimes criticised for attending many functions alone – for like many of his countrymen he possessed a pleasant tenor voice and enjoyed entertaining – but the mores of the day were not to be breached too often and in any case his beloved preferred home life.

On one occasion Moore visited Chatsworth House as a guest of the Duke of Devonshire and hugely enjoyed the experience. Again he went alone and later writing to his mother in Dublin, remarked that he wished Bessie had been with him, "but I knew she would not have been comfortable."

The esteem in which Byron held the Irishman was borne out when he entrusted Moore with his memoirs while the two spent some time together in Venice, two or three years after Moore left Ashbourne. Byron died in 1824 in Greece and the memoirs were burned in a controversial incident but the subsequent biography Moore wrote came to be regarded by many as perhaps his finest work. Many chastised him for his role in that censorious action, but the biography, by ignoring its subject's scandalous private lifestyle – "Mad, bad, and dangerous to know" – ensured Byron's dominant position in the literary world remained quite rightly more important than the salacious episodes.

In 1817 Thomas Moore closed the cottage door for the last time and departed with his family. From Venice on 31 March Byron had written, "I don't know whether to be glad or sorry

St Oswald's church, Ashbourne

that you are leaving Mayfield. Had I been at Newstead during your stay there . . . we should have been within hail, and I should like to have made a giro* of the Peak with you. I know that country well, having been all over it when a boy."

The cottage still stands, now called Tom Moore's Cottage. There are other memories of his stay. Of course, the glorious sounds of St. Oswald's bells delight all who hear them. But there had been great sadness during his stay and in the full version of "*Those Evening Bells*" some have seen reflected something of the sorrow Moore suffered by the tragically early death of his second daughter. Just inside the gateway to Mayfield's parish church of St. John the Baptist stands a headstone, a little apart from the others, its message as brief as the life it recalls, "*Olivia Byron Moore, Born August 18, 1814, Died March 16, 1815*". Byron was her godfather.

For all his love of his own country and a patriotism that swelled with the years away, Thomas Moore was not buried in Ireland. He died in February 1852 in his Wiltshire home at Bromham near Devizes, his mind gone and the five children he so dearly loved all dead. Bessie outlived him, loving him to the end. Moore's grave is marked by a tall cross in Bromham churchyard and within the church the visitor will find a memorial window, raised by public subscription.

* *a round, circuit (Italian)*

2

Enter The Count

One chilly night in the early Fifties I stood, like many other Derby people did that week, in a long queue shuffling towards the Hippodrome in Green Lane. In those days still a theatre, although never quite able to pull in the star names and the big shows, perhaps even then unknowingly resigned to its eventual dreary fate, a bingo hall. That week, however, full houses were assured for the lead, for once, was a well-known name indeed. None other than Hollywood's master of horror, Bela Lugosi, and moreover playing the role on which his fame rested (and damned by, from what we learned later). Count Dracula, Prince of the Vampires.

Lugosi had turned seventy when he brought his strolling players to Derby. The play followed the familiar lines, urged along by a few planted screams among the audience, suggestions of blood-letting on a grand scale and the chilly nightmare of the undead. But the star had passed his limited best and the company wore an air of tiredness. They had done it all before. Soon they would pack their trunks again and go on their way to another town, another theatre, their only stock in trade the name of the elderly man who portrayed the evil and supernatural Transylvanian aristocrat. Lugosi died in 1956, almost an anachronism.

Odd, though, that the production took place at the Hippodrome and not a little further down the road at the Grand Theatre in Babington Lane. For there in 1924 the curtain rose on the world's first-ever staging of Bram Stoker's enduring tale of terror. There must have been some reason for not doing the obvious. From a publicist's viewpoint having the most famous name connected with the title role gliding over the same stage for the first production, the link was the answer to a prayer.

There had been no particular reason why Derby had the honour of that first production. Actor/manager Hamilton Deane had adapted Stoker's book some time before and decided to try it out while his company was in town for a two-week run at the Grand, armed with three plays. Deane and his players were regular visitors and popular with local theatre-goers, usually presenting firmly established fare. He decided that the last three nights of the programme would be taken up by *Dracula.*

And on 15 May the blood-feasting Count unfurled his bat-wings for his world stage debut. It is a matter of theatrical statistics that the play nearly always proved a crowd-pleaser although companies rarely perform it nowadays. The cinema, with its capacity to underline the gory chronicle with blood smears a yard wide, has virtually killed off stage presentations. Deane's version did well for the limited run and the Derby newspaper's theatre critic duly noted:

> "While under the spell of the breathless action and excellent acting one forgets the absolute twaddle to which one is listening. The utter drivel of were-wolves, vampires, and the undead, which provokes nothing but laughter in the sane light of day, becomes dreadful reality in the semi-darkness of the stage."

"Twaddle" maybe, but Deane had permitted his baptismal Derby audience a view of a supernatural and evil underworld and who among them, in an honest moment, would have denied the vicarious thrill it afforded? Many years before Byron had sensed the attraction:

But first on earth, as vampire sent,
Thy corpse from its tomb be rent,
Then ghastly haunt thy native place
And suck the blood of all thy race.

Deane played the part of Dr van Helsing, pursuer of Dracula, in turn played by one Edmund Blake, a name forgotten in theatre history.

Notwithstanding there already being a film version (the truly spooky 1922 German silent production *Nesferatu* whose translation reads "*The Undead*", the title originally favoured by Stoker) the stage *Dracula* enjoyed phenomenal success. After Derby Hamilton Deane took it to other towns and more full houses thrilled to the mysterious count with the white face, blood-red eyes and satanic wig. Deane needed no convincing that he had a winner. London beckoned and in 1927 the West End saw for itself the strange play which had so enthralled provincial audiences. Critics savaged the production which should have been the kiss of death but, as the Count's incisor kiss ensured immortality of a sort for his victims, the play survived and enjoyed hit status in the capital. By then the "Derby version" had undergone some changes. Deane, with another theatrical, John Balderston, had re-worked the original for the London run and it is that joint version which generally came to be used by theatre companies the world over.

Bram Stoker appears as a most unlikely candidate to have written a horror classic which since the first edition in 1897 has never been out of print. An Irishman possessed of a magnificent physique and boundless energy, he was born in Dublin in 1847, baptised Abraham but known to one and all as Bram.

Graduating from Dublin's Trinity College, Stoker threw himself into the fullest of lives. Qualifying as a barrister at London's Inner Temple, in his sixty-four years of life he pursued other careers: civil servant, journalist, newspaper editor, short story writer, theatrical secretary and, of course, novelist. His first published work was far removed from his awesome creation. *The Duties of Clerks of Petty Sessions* was written while employed as a civil servant in Dublin and at least possessed the merit of assured sales.

The old Grand Theatre, Derby

An odd note in Stoker's career is that no less a public figure than H.M. Stanley encouraged him to take up writing seriously. The man who tracked down the lost Livingstone had read a pamphlet on North America written by the Irishman was impressed and told him so. And so a career was born.

Writing apart, Stoker had always been fascinated by the theatre and at Birmingham in 1878 met the actor Henry Irving. From that meeting the greatest actor of the day gained a highly efficient and utterly devoted secretary. Irving died in 1905 and in those twenty-seven years he stretched his secretary to the full. Stoker drew on his vast reservoir of energy and when theatrical duties allowed, wrote his novels.

None ever matched *Dracula*. Nowadays the name of Bram Stoker might encourage those seeking further grisly thrills to read *The Lady of the Shroud* or *The Lair of the White Worm*. They will most likely find themselves disappointed for neither remotely approached the fatal lure of *Dracula*. Even that Gothic masterpiece drags in places, its enduring popularity owing much to the truly nightmarish opening chapters. Thought to have been written in haste they nevertheless, even after all these years, rarely fail to arouse in the reader a shudder of cold unease.

Stoker has a further but more tenuous association with Derbyshire. Some years ago they filmed *The Lair of the White Worm* but the production earned only slight critical approval although it has since become something of a cult film. Parts of the book and the film are set in the Peak District but, location apart, neither has much to recommend it.

3

The Resurrection Men

The setting could not have been better. Two hours beyond midnight and two men riding a gig passed rapidly through the toll bar, demanding of the keeper that he keep the bar raised for their journey back. Sometime later the light two-wheeled carriage returned, its horse still being urged along at a rapid rate. The men, smoking cigars now, berated the keeper for having, despite their request, lowered the bar and so slowing down their retreat. Their cursing done the strangers whipped their horse and clattered off into the darkness of the night, clearly anxious to be gone. They were carrying an extra, unseen passenger who lay very still indeed.

Later that Thursday the toll bar keeper had cause to remember the night travellers. There was talk in Eckington village, lying to the north of Chesterfield, that a new grave in the graveyard of the SS Peter and Paul church had been tampered with. Anxious to learn the truth, villagers re-opened the grave and their worst suspicions were confirmed. The body of Ann Allen, daughter of the landlord of the White Hart Inn across the road from the church, had disappeared. Presumably her father was the Job Allen recorded as being landlord there in 1795. She had been buried on Monday, 4 December 1828, and by Thursday had become a victim of the body-snatchers, grimly nicknamed the Resurrection or "sack-'em up" men. There was no doubt the two who cursed so roundly as they rattled through Mosborough toll were the offenders, engaged in a trade then at its height. A weathered gravestone lies at Eckington with the name Job Allen recorded as having died in what looks like 1846; there is no Ann Allen named.

Body-snatching has a history going back many centuries and anywhere where surgeons and anatomists needed cadavers on which to conduct research and discover the miracles of the human body and pass that knowledge on to their students. In Britain the bodies of hanged criminals were a constant source for there were so many offences for which one could be hanged that the dissecting tables were reasonably well-provided for. Another source was the destitute for whom no relations came to claim their bodies for a decent burial. Before the passing of the 1832 Anatomy Act there existed no formal requirement for training or a licence and anyone could set up shop as an anatomist.

Researchers tend to date the start of the Resurrection Era to 1742 when the supply of cadavers from the gallows started to decline following the lessening of capital offences. This falling off heralded the emergence of highly organised gangs led by men with a sharp business sense, sufficiently so that when the disgusting trafficking came to an end some were able to retreat into comfortable retirement. In 1752 an Act of Parliament decreed that executed murderers' bodies be handed over for dissection, although families were sometimes able to thwart the authorities. However one views this revolting business, there is no denying that it served its market well and we all have benefited. Body-snatchers were necessary since authority preferred to ignore the fast-growing demands of medical science. Surgeons and anatomists needed fresh corpses and were prepared to pay and handsomely. Their source was of little consequence

In terms of exhuming bodies, the Eckington body-snatchers were slow off the mark. Far swifter the gang that many years before and at the other end of Derbyshire had bagged their prize within a day or so of burial. George Ashmore, described as a "bace coiner of Ashbourne," had as his workshop a cave hewn out of the rock on which stood the Royal Oak public house, close by the pig market. Above ground the counterfeiter co-habited with the landlady. She displayed no compunction at turning over her lover to the authorities when his illegal activities qualified him for the posting of a handsome reward notice. Charged with issuing counterfeit guineas and crowns, Ashmore was found guilty at Derby Assizes in August 1740 and he duly hanged on 4 September.

The Derby Mercury informed its readers that the day following Ashmore's remains "were decently interred by his relations" in the churchyard at Sutton-on-the-Hill. Suspicions were aroused shortly after when observant villagers noticed the newly occupied grave had been disturbed. Shovels were called for and they revealed just an empty coffin and a shroud. That they remained was the trademark of the body-snatcher. As the law stood, to remove a corpse naked was considered a misdemeanour. To take its shroud and coffin as well raised the offence to the status of felony, a much more serious matter! Reminders of George Ashmore's activities surfaced many years later when the Royal Oak, standing at the northern corner of Ashbourne's King Street and Buxton Road was demolished, exposing the cave he had used for his criminal enterprise.

By the time of Ann Allen's exhumation, body-snatching had become furtively widespread. Business had never been better, the gangs never busier. The burgeoning demands were epitomised in London and Edinburgh with their great hospitals and teaching schools. In the same year Ann died the unholy alliance of Burke and Hare was committing its own particular horrors in the stews of the Scottish capital. Strictly speaking, they never qualified as resurrectionists. As far as is known not once did they venture out into the dark night, lanterns and shovels carefully concealed beneath greatcoats, to plunder some remote graveyard. They murdered sixteen or more down and outs in their year of terror, mostly on the

High Bradfield watch-house

premises of their cheap boarding houses, or "but and bens." Little wonder that with such fresh specimens their services were much in demand by the anatomists. When arrested, caught almost accidently, the two Irishmen were about to embark on the importation of corpses from Ireland for there already existed a brisk and well-organised export-import trade between Dublin and Glasgow.

How prevalent body-snatching was in Derbyshire is impossible to decide. Those who earned their living in such appalling fashion were extremely careful to take every precaution; exhumation and removal demanded careful attention to detail. All evidence of a "sack 'em up" had to be eliminated. How successful they could be was displayed some years ago when a disused graveyard in Scotland was dismantled and discovered that some two dozen burial plots contained no human remains. No one had ever been the wiser. On one occasion the Resurrectionists actually struck before the burial service had been conducted.

Prevention of these violations occupied the minds of many. Any suggestion of the use of quick lime drew frowns from the Church, it being considered a bar to eternal life. Iron coffins, massively gated vaults, table tombs, all were tried, but not always attended by success. Up in Edinburgh the iron cages, or "mort safes," can still be seen. They were moved from grave to grave until nature rendered their presence unnecessary. In a report on the Ann Allen "resurrection" it was revealed that iron bars were being used in vaults to clamp down resident coffins.

Families would take turns or maybe hire others to keep watch. Parishes raised funds to build special houses alongside graveyards to accommodate watchers. Just across the Derbyshire border and to the west of Sheffield stands perhaps the finest example of a watch house in England, in the churchyard at High Bradfield. Its original purpose has long since been served and to-day the carefully maintained building serves as an attractive if somewhat unconventional private residence.

For ninety years the Resurrection Men plied their abominable craft. Despite the natural anxiety of bereaved families as well as general revulsion it took authority, as tardy then as now, a long time to do something effective. Burke and Hare proved too much. In 1832 the much-needed Anatomy Act, with its provisions for supplying the anatomists and teaching schools, brought to an abrupt end a sordid but essential trade.

4

An Old Industry

Do you ever pause to consider what a bustling and varied industrial scene Derbyshire must have presented in the last century, particularly its earlier years? There is no need to look far to discover how enormously the Industrial Revolution had affected the county. Evidence is everywhere, such as in the lead ore smelting furnace at Stone Edge dating from the 1770s, now marked by its lonesome free-standing chimney; or the giant beam engine at Middleton Top near Wirksworth. It's just a matter of looking. Starting around the middle of the 18th-century and effectively running for a hundred years the great upheaval transformed England, particularly in the North, from an essentially rural society into an urban industrialised state.

Most people would regard Derbyshire as predominantly rural with industrialised areas confined mainly to its eastern regions. And yet there are ample remains indicating that the Revolution's influence sprawled all over, certainly not least into that epitome of the English countryside the present-day Peak National Park, Britain's first.

There were canals, railways, lead mines and coal mines, and quarries. Alongside, mills produced a whole range from foodstuffs to cotton and silk goods. Factories attached themselves to canals and railways or drawing primitive power from swiftly-running rivers. All combined to make for a regular ants' nest of activity. Much has returned to its former rural condition and it is difficult to envisage what we would have seen, walking our beloved footpaths in those revolutionary times. Which must go some way to explain the rising interest in industrial archaeology. In this county there is so much to seek out and ponder over.

My own particular place in Derbyshire is Stanage Edge. The first visit to an area which on wild winter days can be as awesome as the remotest highlands, was as a schoolboy. The attraction was immediate and has never palled. Nothing can sever the cord which draws me back to that beautiful place. Not even the almost permanent moving population of walkers and climbers not to mention those who challenge the unknown by venturing the odd half mile or so from that universal first base, the car park.

Millstones at Stanage Edge

And, of course, I have seen and sketched those abandoned powerful gritstone wheels peppered here and there beneath Stanage's black beetling edge. With the occasional flight of fancy permitted to us all, I have transformed those huge shaped stones, so neatly holed, from the detritus of an industry with roots far, far older than the Industrial Revolution, into mysterious and thought-provoking abandoned remnants of some long-lost civilisation. A minor primitive version of those colossal statues which imbue remote Easter Island with such mystery! The Long Causeway, that ancient track cutting through the Edge on its sinuous journey from the old Roman camp at Navio (Brough) to Sheffield, would be the sacred route of priests.

What a pity we know so much about those wheels. If we were in ignorance, what a tourist attraction they might become. Hundreds tramping across the moors to gaze on them, to speculate why some had holes in the middle and others not. To ruminate on what cataclysmic event caused their sudden abandonment, some clearly at a time when craftsmen armed with the simplest of tools had just begun to fashion them from raw material torn out of the edge which holds sway over the whole scene. Were they relics of a long-forgotten religion or, more prosaic, an everyday artefact with a function experts had yet to divine? Could they have been destined for an elaborate lunar observatory; or perhaps a temple where a forgotten people wrestled with the eternal vexing question: what is it all about?

Alas, no such intriguing doubts linger over the purpose of those great wheels. Too much is known about them, for what they were intended and of the people who toiled in a hard, demanding and dangerous industry. In their simple way each represents the final form of a basic machine which started off in pre-historic times as the simple quern for grinding the corn. Evolution led to the mill wheel with its improved efficiency and productivity.

Walking among the dozens of millstones beneath Stanage

escarpment, some lying alone half buried in bracken, others in neat sliced rows looking like a cut Swiss roll, the visitor might be forgiven for thinking that here once was a centre of a major industry. Diameters vary from three or four feet to impressive examples over seven feet. Thickness is around a foot, with two tons the average weight. The truth is that there were few places in Derbyshire's northern reaches where gritstone of the necessary texture could be quarried. Stanage overlooks the greatest concentration of relics of an industry which enjoyed boom times with the rising of the Industrial Revolution until more refined machinery replaced those simple stone wheels. Thereafter the old trade dwindled, although it was possible to witness them being produced well into this century.

The wheels were employed in many ways. Grinding corn, pulping wood, grinding cork for linoleum. The paint industry bought them; Derbyshire's hundreds of lead mines were regular customers and occasional discarded wheels are to be found scattered around the abandoned shafts, their ore-crushing days long past. A smaller wheel hewn from Stanage rock went to the cutlers and toolmakers of Sheffield until, once again, cheaper technology pushed out a tool whose roots had witnessed the dawn of history.

Now all that remains are abandoned millstones and the rarer grindstone. Tracks once used to transport them for destinations as far away as Europe now carry the walker and the climber anxious to hone their skills on the challenging face of Stanage.

5

Trouble at t'mill

"I have seen the time when two hand-vices of a pound weight each, more or less, have been screwed to my ears, at Litton Mill in Derbyshire. These are the scars still remaining behind my ears. Then three or four of us have been hung at once on a cross-beam above the machinery, hanging by our hands, without shirts or stockings. Then we used to stand up, in a skip, without our shirts, and be beaten with straps or sticks; the skip was to prevent us running away from the straps . . . Then they used to tie up a 28-pounds weight, one or two at once, according to our size, to hang down our backs, with no shirt on."

An advertisement in a May 1793 edition of the *Derby Mercury* offered a reward, together with reimbursement of any expenses incurred, for the apprehension of two apprentices who had absconded from the cotton mill at Litton. The boy was David Powell, aged about thirteen, and Mary Bedingfield, his companion, a year older and described as dark of complexion and hair and having "remarkably thick lips."

In 1975 the *Derby Evening Telegraph* reviewed a book which dealt in minute detail with malpractices which once held sway at Litton.

Clearly there had been "trouble at t'mill" on a grand scale.

* * *

Litton Mill

A well-rewarded walk is the one which starts out at Tideswell, follows the road up to Litton village – the mill itself is not there – and then takes to the fields to eventually drop down to Ravensdale. A turn or two brings the hiker to the remains of Cressbrook Mill, a handsome edifice even in obsolescence and time-ravaged. Built in 1815 by William Newton, the "Minstrel of the Peak," the mill signals the start of the walk's most attractive stretch. Here one meets up with the River Wye flowing through the delightful Water-cum-Jolly dale. Limestone cliffs bear down on deep, clear waters, or watch the river in more playful mood tumbling over weirs. In spring there is a riot of wild flowers and the birds' chorus completes the magic of this short, wooded valley.

Towards the end of Water-cum-Jolly rise the grey buildings of Litton Mill. Not the one already referred to, that was razed by fire in 1874 although remains can be found. However, the memory of that dreadful first mill lingers on. Several guide books make reference to the brutality suffered by parish apprentices bound there. "Child slavery at its worst," one affirms.

Ellis Needham and Thomas Frith, two local men, built the original mill around 1782. Events would prove they were too optimistic with their venture into cotton; Litton was too remote and under-funded. For the first few years, however, the partners did quite well, but the inevitable decline set in. They put the business up for sale in 1786 but no one displayed any interest. Frith pulled out in 1799 to leave the parsimonious Needham, with his son John, to get by as best they may. Their efforts proved no match against mounting odds: depression in the cotton trade, a mill fire, a crippled water wheel. By 1815 Needham was a broken man, bankrupt and forced to move out.

Even in the mills of more enlightened owners life was hard and the hours tediously long. For those employed at Litton conditions could only be the grimmest as Needham struggled against the rising tide. Most of his labour force were apprentices from parish workhouses, many orphaned and little more than children. The youngsters, boys and girls, were cheap and plentiful and consequently welcomed by mill owners. The more unscrupulous would let some go before completing their time, to become a burden on the parish. More would then be recruited. Child slavery might be too strong a term, but in some instances almost apposite.

That Ellis Needham and Litton Mill did not slip into the oblivion to which they were doomed is due entirely to one man. A Londoner, illegitimate Robert Blincoe was born around 1792 and placed in the St. Pancras workhouse. There he remained until seven when, along with others in the same boat, he was shipped off to Nottingham to serve as a parish apprentice at Lambert's cotton mill at Lowdham. Once he attempted to run away but was caught and flogged. The lesson learned, he stayed until the mill closed in 1803 and then moved, with other apprentices, to remote Litton. Young Robert remained there for four years.

No doubt the young London apprentice did suffer. Blincoe in later years would describe how he and his companions were maltreated at Water-cum-Jolly. So extensive and detailed is the catalogue that the reader might wonder just what sort of business Needham was really in. Were Blincoe and others dished out such treatment by mill supervisors *pour encourager les autres*? Little wonder David Powell and Mary Bedingfield chose to run away.

According to Blincoe, feeding was a disgusting procedure. Staple diet consisted mostly of water-porridge and oat cakes, bacon broth and unpared turnips, or rice "full of maggots" boiled in bags. Hardly surprising that knives, forks and spoons were not provided. Youngsters fancying further helpings of some revolting mess helped themselves by grubbing through the mill's dunghill hoping to scratch out cabbage leaves or maybe potato and turnip parings.

Accommodation was crowded and abysmal, filthy and foul-smelling; working hours mercilessly long. Fridays were earmarked for washing. Vermin lodging in an apprentice's hair would be painfully removed by placing a pitch cap on the offending head and then torn off.

Nauseous and obscene, Blincoe's litany is a terrible indictment of Ellis Needham and his unfortunate cotton mill. Brutality the order of the day; the death rate among apprentices unusually high. Those who attempted to abscond had their legs strapped in irons similar to those rivetted on felons.

And then the thought arises: does not Robert Blincoe protest *too* much?

Remember, his account at Litton Mill is the only detailed one available. True there were inspectors' reports which described conditions as somewhat frugal and noted that some regulations were being ignored to the detriment of apprentices. Such would not have been unique to Litton. But nothing to back up Blincoe's catalogue of cruelties. Nor do contemporary records sustain the claim of an unduly high death rate.

Notwithstanding all those abuses, the most extraordinary feature of Blincoe's story is that he did not feel moved to tell it until 1822, *fifteen* years after walking through the gates of Litton Mill to seek a living, his apprenticeship served. By then he ran a small grocery shop in Manchester as well as dealing in cotton waste. Even more extraordinary is that Blincoe's account was not published until 1828, twenty-one years after the Litton days. By then his motive could hardly have been revenge on Ellis Needham since that unfortunate had sold out, a broken man, thirteen years earlier and, according to reports, was later reduced to a pauper.

Robert Blincoe first spoke to John Brown, a Bolton-born journalist surely lacking in basic professional instincts for he does not appear to have made any attempt to publish such a sensational story. He committed suicide in 1825. When the story finally came out it was through the pages of *The Lion* a publication devoted to the cause of factory reform. Such was the interest and anger spawned by the report that two reprints followed within twelve months.

In 1832, by then forty years old and twenty-five years after quitting Litton, Blincoe's story was published yet again, this time by John Doherty, founder of the National Union of Cotton Spinners, under the comprehensive title, *A Memoir of Robert Blincoe, An Orphan Boy; sent from the workhouse of St. Pancras, London, at seven years of age, to endure the Horrors of a Cotton-Mill, through his infancy and youth, with a minute detail of his sufferings*. (It was that publication, with slight amendments, which reappeared as a reprint in 1975 and reviewed in Derby's evening newspaper). The following year Blincoe repeated his story, but this time in person and before the Government's Central Board on Employment of Children in Manufacturies. What he had to say became incorporated within an official report and to-day resides within the Parliamentary Papers of 1833. (The opening quotation is extracted from that report).

In evidence, he claimed that while at Litton his body was never free from contusions or wounds. The ex-apprentice backed up that statement by showing his listeners still-visible body scars and a deformed knee. In an obvious parallel with the black slaves of the American cotton fields, Blincoe called children employed in England's cotton mills "white infant-slaves." Allowing his experiences to be published was, he explained, "for the protection of the rising generation of factory children."

So, while we seek out the remains along Water-cum-Jolly of Needham's satanic mill, what can be made of Blincoe's startling, if somewhat tardy, revelations? All those years before he spoke out and then to be received at face value without corroboration of any sort. Nor, equally significant, any refutation. In its day the recital caused a mighty uproar and, in general, has been accepted over the years.

The answer to the apparent riddle may lie in part with the antagonism existing between established farming interests and the increasing encroachments of mill owners. Farmers saw a threat to the pool of cheap and plentiful labour they enjoyed. Needham himself proved unpopular by pre-releasing many of his apprentices, to become a burden on parish funds. So much so that local farmers petitioned Lord Scarsdale over the matter. This led to Needham being given notice to quit and bankruptcy finished his sad tale at Litton. And eighty more apprentices were thrown on the parish.

Then there was the crusade for factory reform led by men such as the Welsh socialist and philanthropist Robert Owen, himself a former mill manager and inspiration for the revolutionary co-operative movement. That Robert Blincoe did suffer at Litton may be accepted, but because his testimony remains unsupported we cannot be certain as to its authority or credibility. Nor can the running away by two apprentices be regarded as profoundly significant; such dashes for freedom were not uncommon.

Publication of Blincoe's dreadful experiences should have provided a fine propaganda weapon with which to fight for reform in the cotton industry, and there is ample evidence that there had been abuse of young, cheap labour. But a weapon by then nearly a quarter of a century old? Was there nothing more contemporary, more relevant to the times for reformers to recruit to their worthy crusade? Might it not be inferred that abuses were much less and factory conditions much improved since Ellis Needham ruled at Litton? Evidence suggests they were.

Significant is that Blincoe's extraordinary revelations did not persuade others to come forward and offer up their experiences. Their not doing so casts Blincoe in the role of a man who had suffered uniquely; his publication a twist on the story of the dog that did not bark. Here one must ask why it took so long to do so.

A

MEMOIR

OF

ROBERT BLINCOE,

An Orphan Boy;

SENT FROM THE WORKHOUSE OF ST. PANCRAS, LONDON,

AT SEVEN YEARS OF AGE,

TO ENDURE THE

Horrors of a Cotton-Mill,

THROUGH HIS INFANCY AND YOUTH,

WITH A MINUTE DETAIL OF HIS SUFFERINGS,

BEING

THE FIRST MEMOIR OF THE KIND PUBLISHED.

BY JOHN BROWN.

MANCHESTER:

PRINTED FOR AND PUBLISHED BY J. DOHERTY, 37, WITHY-GROVE.

1832.

6

Where the Tide Turned

Many would regard Bonnie Prince Charlie's advance on Derby and subsequent retreat as that city's historical highlight. An interesting debate would be what event would replace it had the Young Pretender manage to overrule his military advisers and continued the swift advance on London in his daring bid to wrest the English throne from the Hanovarians in the shape of George II. While Derby has a most worthy and long history, nothing remotely approaches those three astonishing days in December 1745 when the course of a nation might have changed.

As a young lad I grew up with the story of how Charlie's Highland horde reached Derby and then detached an advance party with orders to secure Swarkestone Bridge, essential to their advance on the capital. It was the one item of local history I felt secure about. I lived not too far from the bridge, just a pleasant stroll through the fields and across a canal. That long stone bridge across the River Trent proved the southern-most point the Scottish army reached, with the advance guard camping on the northern bank somewhere among the present-day homes of Swarkestone village. A picquet, sixty or seventy strong, was detailed to move across the bridge and take possession of Stanton-by-Bridge.

Strictly speaking, the award of furthest south for the Jacobite advance should be moved from Derby's grasp and be placed with Loughborough in Leicestershire, a town reached by a party of the Prince's officers in a quest for support for the Stuart cause. Logic supports the claim that Charles himself rode south of his advance guards, crossing the Trent to speak with Sir Henry Harpur at Calke Abbey and Sir Robert Burdett at Foremark Hall in an attempt to add their influential weight to the stupendous adventure.

Swarkestone Bridge

One of the truly stirring episodes in this island's history, Prince Charles Edward Stuart's lightning campaign to depose Hanover's George II and restore the House of Stuart in the person of King James III, his father, started off on the remote western coast of Scotland at Glenfinnan late 1745. At the head of his Highlanders and a strong contingent of Irish from the French army Charles swept southwards, winning all before him. What many dismissed as a hopeless enterprise assumed a more ominous air when the invaders poured over the border into England and captured Carlisle. Suddenly alarm bells were ringing. In London a tide of panic began to rise and before Derby had been reached George II had fully prepared himself for ignominious flight to the continent.

How much loyalty Charles could attract and how much George could retain were always questionable quantities. With the facts nowadays available there is every reason to think the Bonnie Prince had far more chance than his advisers in Derby credited him with. Had they been aware how worried the Duke of Cumberland, commanding the Government forces and well-nicknamed "the Butcher," was over the seemingly inexorable advance, Swarkestone's bridge might then have carried the full weight of a seven thousand-strong army marching on to London. "The whole kingdom is asleep," snapped Cumberland in a report, furious at the Government's lack of response to an increasingly dangerous situation.

Bonnie Prince Charlie first saw Derbyshire at Ashbourne, where his father was proclaimed King. On 4 December, 1745 he entered Derby. A tall, charismatic figure, vigorous and handsome, not quite twenty-five years. His army of seven thousand and followers numbering another two thousand more than doubled the market town's population. Charles lodged at Exeter House in Full Street while his senior officers took over the houses of the gentry. Billets were sought for the troops while recruits were sought among the citizens, though with little success. The heavy artillery was stationed at Nuns Green (to-day's Friar Gate).

While the *Derby Mercury* would later report the hectic three days of Charles' stay in slighting terms, there is no question that the Jacobites, "marked with dirt and fatigue," generally were well-received and, on the whole, the invading troops behaved themselves. They hardly deserved the description published afterwards in the *Mercury*:

> "Most of them are a parcel of shabby, lousy, pitiful-look'd fellows, mix'd up with old men and boys; dress'd in dirty

plaids and as dirty shirts, without breeches and wore their stockings made of plaid not much above half way up their legs and some without shoes or next to none and numbers of them so fatigu'd with their long march, that they commanded our pity rather than our fear."

Derby people, according to the newspaper, concluded that those who did not speak English (quite a few), conversed in "wild Irish." Clearly forgotten by the reporter were the victories *en route*, the twenty-four hour forced march to Derby completing a brilliant out-flanking movement which left Cumberland flat-footed and bewildered too far west.

Some of Derby's leaders had already quit the scene. The mayor had left town, so too the town clerk. Magistrates and other prominent figures made themselves more prominent by their scampered absence. Before the rising sun of the Jacobites' advance melted its military ardour Derby had taken measures to defend itself. Under the Duke of Devonshire's leadership a force numbering seven hundred was raised, to be known as the Derby Regiment, otherwise the "Derby Blues."

On 3 December the regiment performed certain military exercises and reportedly gave "great satisfaction." Then came the stunning news that the invaders had actually arrived in Ashbourne. With commendable speed the "Blues" re-assembled, armed themselves with torches and marched off to Nottingham. The Duke led the way. Presumably military appreciation had worked out that the Prince's route lay south, not east. To make doubly sure of eluding the "shabby, lousy, pitiful-look'd fellows," Derby's defenders swung north from Nottingham and advanced on Mansfield. And there they remained until Charles' council of war had carried out the fateful decision to retreat.

A more creditable effort came from the good people of Weston-on-Trent. News of the Scots' presence in Derby had reached nearby Swarkestone, whose inhabitants understandable first reaction was to hide anything of value. Further south the people of Melbourne prepared to welcome the Jacobites. Weston men were made of sterner stuff, fully prepared if not so equipped to defend their village or at least volunteer a hand in any general resistance. A hurriedly convened meeting despatched three men to learn if the Jacobites might come their way. Meanwhile William Rose, blacksmith, was ordered to repair the "town musquet" at a cost of one shilling and the meeting authorised a further one shilling and sixpence for the purchase of powder. As the "Derby Blues" marched off to the east, Weston lay in readiness.

While those soldiers despatched to secure Swarkestone Bridge passed quite close to the village on 4 December, and Prince Charles himself might have done the same next day, there is no record that Weston's gallant few ever clapped eyes on the enemy. But they were prepared to fight and when danger had passed the villagers quite rightly voted themselves a day of thanksgiving.

Charles and his advisers spent 5 December in a flurry of activity, the most important item on the agenda being a council as to whether or not to advance. Charles naturally advocated pressing on, to go with the tide that had placed the Highlanders little more than a hundred miles from London. Lord George Murray, his military commander, counselled retreat. Both men were hindered by a lack of intelligence reports. Nobody knew for sure where the Government's armies lay and in what strength. Charles was too optimistic, Murray too pessimistic. Murray carried the day, leaving the Prince helpless and fuming. Only when the whole venture was subjected to historical analysis did it emerge that the Jacobite thrust south had been so swift that Government forces were, even from Derby, too far away and not well-organised. Cumberland lay to the west, unable to quickly frustrate the invaders. London's streets might have echoed to the march of invaders' feet before the "Butcher" caught up and by then the tide maybe flowing too strongly against the House of Hanover. General Wade lay away to the north, rendered ineffective by distance. The road from Derby to London itself was poorly defended and the capital moreover seized by foreboding when the alarming news got through of just who had arrived so close as Derby.

But it was not to be. On 6 December the invaders quit Derby, to commence the long retreat to Scotland and murderous humiliation at Culloden moor the following April, one of the most shameful episodes in British military history. Bonnie Prince Charles had triumphantly led his main force into Derby two days before. On the third day he left, bringing up the rear. His tragic decline, physical and psychological, had begun. "Black Friday" is how the Jacobite annals named that awful day.

Just three Derby men had volunteered to join the invaders and they soon deserted. One was John Sparks, a stocking-maker. As the disillusioned Highlanders trooped towards Ashbourne Sparks dropped out, only to be discovered by the authorities drunk in the wine cellars of Hugo Meynell's house at Bradley. Arrested, he was later executed

Derby remembers the stirring events of The '45 in several ways. Plaques here and there recall significant sites and recent years have witnessed a gaily-costumed parade early each December celebrating the triumphant arrival of the Prince. In 1945, the two-hundreth anniversary of the invasion, a memorial tablet was unveiled in Derby cathedral to commemorate the special church service held there for the Stuarts. Newspaper reports hint there may have been reservations over the occasion. Some Derbyshire families said to have been prominent in their opposition to the Catholic Stuarts' cause, "expressed their approval of this important episode in the history of Derby." Reading the accounts of those three tumultuous, welcoming days and the deployment of the Derby "Blues", one might reasonably query where the opposition lay. Charles moved without hindrance through

Derbyshire. Only the villagers of Weston are recorded as having done anything positive, even if only to prime the "town musquet." Latent support for the Young Pretender may have been quietly in place, just waiting for a safer moment to manifest itself.

An interesting momento of the Highlanders dramatic arrival is a street ballad which appeared, like the "Blues," shortly after their departure, a note of which appeared under the year 1820 in a scrap-book kept by the Dowager Lady Sitwell. At that time, there lived in the village of Mappleton an old woman who, despite declining faculties, could still quote passages of a song first heard in her childhood:

When this rebellious crew
They unto Derby drew
Which did affright
The people to behold
The rebels were so bold
They said "We have your gold
And all your land"
They wheeled to and fro
But could no further go
Who must their leader be?
One of the rebels, he
Said "Arm up and follow me
You Highland lads."
O! Then with sword in hand
As we do understand
By the Duke of Perth's command
O! Send their bones some plaid
O! Send oatmeal besade
Two nights and days they staid
This scurvy host
In popery I'm but young
That did compose this song

But yet my heart and tongue
Both do agree
And pray the loving Lord
That sends us daily food
None of the popish brood
Shall rule the road.

7

The Princess and The Wolves

Though not in Derbyshire, the east Staffordshire village of Ilam is sufficiently close to deserve inclusion in this collection. Nestling at the foot of the Pennines the attractive estate village, west of where the rivers Manifold and Dove are in conjunction, is largely a 19th-century creation. Half-timbered and stone-built houses interspersed by green areas and the whole stands on the banks of the crystal-clear waters of the Manifold. Beyond this idyllic setting lies a richly wooded valley deservedly called Paradise.

Jewel in this rural crown is the church of Holy Cross standing primly within its ancient graveyard. A mixture of architectural styles ranging from Saxon to Decorated, the building reveals that Ilam is a far older settlement than suggested by first impressions. Tenth-century crosses adorn the graveyard while just within the church doors stands a Saxon font whose carved stone panels depict scenes easily deciphered despite the passage of centuries. An early Victorian traveller must have failed to translate the carvings for he wrote of the "capacious and curiously-figured font."

The panels show scenes from the life of Saint Bertram, whose impressive but empty stone tomb is the principal feature of a side chapel dedicated to this little-known 7th-century holy man. One panel contains two primitive figures, one of the saint the other his wife. Another contains a gruesome scene, a giant wolf devouring a human head. A chilling carving in such a pleasing church.

The church at Ilam

Early Christian saints were often soldiers or men of noble birth who, for some reason or another, renounced their calling to follow the path of God. Bertram, sometimes Bettelin, reputedly was the son of the Prince of Stafford, a town lying in the heart of the old kingdom of Mercia. Journeying to Ireland he met and fell in love with the beautiful daughter of an Irish king. The prince's son and princess were married, a union that stimulated the anger of her father sufficiently for the young couple to flee the country and make their way to Mercia.

By then the young bride was pregnant and the journey home to Stafford accordingly slow and tedious. As they entered the great forest that covered much of the kingdom, the princess went into labour at a place that to-day is Ilam. Bertram fashioned a rough and ready shelter for his wife while he went to seek out a midwife. While away two things happened, the baby was born and a pack of wolves arrived on the scene. Mother and child were cruelly slain and the prowling hunters gorged themselves in unexpected style.

Bertram would have been well aware of the danger he left his princess in. The English wolf, close cousin to the ferocious European timber wolf, made his home in those forestlands. With its remote hills and dales and deep woods, Derbyshire provided those predators with almost undetectable shelter. Place-names – such as Wolfscote Dale – are memorials to the former presence of those remorseless hunters. Records testify that the wolf could be found there almost to the close of the 18th-century.

Nor would the princess have been unaware of the danger of her situation. In her native Ireland the wolf was a menace not only in fact but, along with the were-wolf, occupied a dominant place in Irish legends. One well-known one told that while Saint Patrick preached Christianity to her country there was one clan, openly hostile to his presence, which possessed the awesome ability to change into wolves and, taking to the woods, hunt for food like the animals they had become.

Returning with a midwife Bertram was horrified by what he discovered. His young wife mutilated to death, so too the baby he had never known not even for a few precious moments. He renounced his royal heritage on the spot where he lost his family and became a hermit. Only once, on the death of his father, did he emerge from his self-imposed isolation. The principality was being threatened by a usurper's army, led by a demon. Appeals to Bertram at Ilam did not go unheeded and, aided by an angel from heaven, he raised a force and defeated Stafford's enemies. Victory secured, Bertram returned to Ilam and continued to follow God to his dying day, around 710AD. Many seeking him out were converted to his Faith, persuaded by his holiness and good works. At his death the hermitage became a shrine and many miracles were attributed to such a sacred place.

An early Victorian local history states that Ilam was noted for the tomb of Saint Bertram, his well high up on Bunster Hill and an ash tree dedicated to him. As for the saint himself he performed many "stupendous miracles" in the county. Local people once venerated the ash tree and regarded it a highly dangerous thing to break a bough off. Sadly the 1839 book, which made no mention of the wolf pack and its victims, revealed that, "Little, however, is now thought of either the saint, or his tomb and well."

All is not quite as it seems with this unhappy story. Anyone probing into the life of Bertram, or Bettelin, will eventually uncover the fact that the tale is almost certainly fictitious. Bettelin is the patron saint of Stafford and precious little is known about him and what is must be examined with caution. The legend of Bertram/Bettelin and the wolves is told with more authority of the French saint Berthleme, of Fecamp in Normandy.

Such revelations lead to the inevitable question, whose body then once occupied that impressive tomb in the side chapel of Holy Cross church? To-day it is extremely unlikely the question will ever be answered, although it may be possible that the tomb came from a long-lost abbey which, records suggest, lay on the western bank of the Manifold upstream from Ilam.

8

Unique – Purpose Unknown

Nikolaus Pevsner pronounced it as "An extremely odd structure," in his definitive work *The Buildings of England*. Few would disagree. Variously, this Jacobean-styled building has been called a folly, a banqueting hall, a cock fighting and bear baiting venue, a jousting field even. The local Harpur family records provide a tantalising clue, for a Richard Shepherd was paid £111 12 4d for building the "bowle alley house" between 1630-32. To further confuse matters, the architect may have been a John Smythson. Whether or not Pevsner's "odd structure" or some other, now long-gone building was the "alley house" is impossible to say. Another building, unidentifiable from the same records, was built some time after 1632.

Commonest identity is the Pavilion, although as mere youngsters scratching and scrambling for birds' eggs within its empty mouldering rooms and hollow towers, we called it the bull-ring. Obviously no one can agree on its original function and since the place is apparently unique, help has not been forthcoming from elsewhere.

The building – let us, too, call it the Pavilion – can be seen off to the left of the A5132, half-hidden among tall trees, just before that road swings sharply south to pass through Swarkestone village and over the historic bridge crossing the

The Pavilion, Swarkestone

River Trent and off to Melbourne. An attractive place, the main body being topped by a gangling chimney and flanked by two towers each supporting a cupola-like roof. Set in the north wall of a stone wall enclosure, its principal entrance, a slightly arched gateway, lets into the opposing south wall. The enclosure itself has been called the Cuttle, an odd name presumably derived from the nearby bridge and brook of that name.

For certain is that the Pavilion and enclosure were the creation of the Harpurs, a prominent local family once residing at nearby Swarkestone Hall, the only remains of which are some lengths of broken wall and a beautifully restored tithe barn. Strongly fancied as the instigator is Sir John Harpur (died 1677). His other, certain, claim on local fame is for leading a Royalist force to defeat against the Roundheads in 1643 during the Civil War when the all-important Swarkestone Bridge became a military objective.

Whatever dreams brought forth the Pavilion, they faded along time's passage and their realisation gradually became the echoing, romantic ivy-clad place of our youth. Residential rooks and permanent pigeons temporarily sought refuge elsewhere when the rock group The Rolling Stones rolled up in the late Sixties, to lounge against doorways and drape through windows in a photographic session for the sleeve design of an eventual best-selling album. After that, more oblivion, with the enclosure serving as an effective cattle fold.

Rescue of this singular place came twenty years later. Increasing awareness of an irreplaceable heritage, even if no one knew quite what in this case, saw money being made available for some fine restoration work. Swarkestone's Pavilion became a unique form of holiday home, a place for gentle pleasure and relaxation. This was probably the original intention of its creator, if the truth be known.

9

When Lola Came to Town

Maybe they opened the doors an hour before the lecture anticipating that Derby's Temperance Hall in Curzon Street would be filled to capacity. After all, the speaker was a most exciting and mysterious women who, as both dancer and actress, had filled the theatres of England, Europe, America and Australia. Her escapades, her lovers, the highly suggestive Spider Dance, had made her name (adopted) or title (of which she had been stripped), common knowledge. Her extraordinary career, on and off stage, ensured her name remained so for many years after her death. She once confessed, "There was not a wicked thing that I did not do . . ." Even now there is a serious attempt to bring out, at long last, a definitive and reliable biography. The authorative *Dictionary of National Biography* is as unreliable as the many other accounts of her life, including her own ghosted autobiographies. For the lady was an incorrigible liar.

Even if the diminutive woman who eventually emerged on the stage had no other talent, it could not be disputed that she was a superb self-publicist and a fine speaker. So much so that, since her death, there have been at least a dozen biographies to supplement her own efforts, two or three ballets about or featuring her, the odd play and in 1954 a major feature film. So far there has been no television presentation, although her story would undoubtedly make for a rumbustious and colourful production.

The Temperance Hall had not filled when, just gone eight o'clock on a cold night in February 1859, the scandalous Lola Montez addressed her audience. Most there, including, so we are told, "a fair sprinkling of highly respectable ladies" of Derby knew her by that name, although she preferred to be addressed by her Bavarian title Countess Landsfeldt, a courtesy to which she had no longer any claim. Such trivialities were little heeded by this beautiful, raven-haired woman born Marie Gilbert around forty years before. Her correct age, where in Ireland she was born (probably Limerick), are among the many mysteries surrounding this wide-eyed siren which were nurtured carefully and have infuriated her several biographers ever since. Other webs she spun included two bigamous marriages – her first husband outlived her – and a couple of deaths in suspicious circumstances.

Lola Montez as a young woman

Derby Mercury's reporter wrote of her erratic (and erotic) career, the runaway marriage to an Indian Army officer at fourteen (actually fifteen), her interference in Bavarian politics while mistress of the monarch, King Ludwig I, the "cowhider" of editors. The latter odd description referred to the time Lola headed off to Australia and its newly-discovered gold fields, two or three years before her Derby appearance. In Victoria at the gold-rush town of Ballarat she took exception to what the local newspaper editor had written about her character and, grabbing a whip, soundly thrashed him in public view. That was in addition to besting a female heckler in a bar-room brawl. What the reporter failed to mention was the tempestuous affair with the pianist and composer Franz Liszt which scandalised Europe and incurred the displeasure of composer Richard Wagner. There were other affairs, one certainly with author Alexander Dumas and possibly Tzar Nicholas I of Russia, but too numerous to mention. A famous duel had been fought over her in Paris. At the end of the day Lola Montez could only be described as courtesan *par excellence.* In present day terms she would have single-handedly kept London's tabloid gutter press happy for years on end and made a considerable fortune while doing so.

The woman who stood on the Temperance Hall stage appeared, as the reporter spitefully noted, somewhat past her best. He could not have known that Montez's health had begun to give cause for concern. Her features were most expressive but "care-worn," her smile pleasing but "no longer fascinating." There was no mention of the dark eyes which would remain beautiful to her dying day. Her dress of black velvet was relieved only by a deep white lace collar fitting close to the throat, a fashion that had always been her most favoured.

Unbeknown to its members, what the Derby audience saw was a woman at the cross-roads of her life. The old days were over; a spiritual metamorphosis had begun. Moreover there is sound evidence that Lola Montez would later give serious thought to settling down in Derbyshire, to live a quiet life and finally come to terms with a troubled mind. Repentance weighed heavily on her soul; her lecture that cold February night had been written by her American mentor, the Reverend Chauncy Burr. There were several talks to be delivered over a lengthy lecture tour that started off in Dublin the previous

November and would not finish until June, in London. Some dealt with beautiful women, others gallantry and history's heroines. For her Derby audience she had chosen to speak on the comic aspects of fashion in Society.

The *Mercury's* representative refused to be captivated by the Countess Landsfeldt. While praising her dramatic skills and elocution, they were not sufficient to redeem the lecture from its "stains of bad taste and bad feeling." There was no elaboration nor explanation, except to condemn the talk as a "rather spiteful and stale assault upon the privileges and practices of that society." Maybe the lady was not in the best of form for her audience that night; in London the following April tickets for four highly successful lectures were more expensive than those to hear Charles Dickens with his popular readings.

Had Montez not returned to Derbyshire later that year then her first visit would have merited no further attention. But return she did and the *Mercury* either chose to ignore the fact or remained unaware of her presence until too late. In early October a few lines told that she had returned to America and reminded readers that she had stayed locally for some time during the summer. There were no other details. In fact Lola had hurried away from Derbyshire during the last few days of September, was in London on 1 October and three days later sailed on the *Harmonia*, bound for New York.

While in London she wrote in her diary, of which only fragments survive, that there had been a dispute in Derby with a man only noted as "Mr E." who had been "cruel indeed . . . to have said what he did; but I am afraid I was too hasty also. Ought I have to resented what was said? No, I ought to have said not a word." Montez's decision to return to America may well have had a bearing on her sad, early death. Without any doubt she regretted that hasty departure, scribbling, "Good-bye to all the calm hours of reflection and repose I enjoyed at Derby! My calm days at the cottage are gone – gone."

10

And the Walls Came Tumbling Down

From an office I had a front row view of the final days of Derby's Manor Hospital in Uttoxeter Road, before the familiar lines of Southmead block came crashing down in February 1992. Each day a little more crumbled from what had been a fine-looking building. Melancholy attends the destruction of buildings, especially those designed by architects and not built by accountants. Like so many Victorian public edifices the Manor reflected style and a sense of proportion no matter the place's purpose. Watching the old place disappear was like watching something dying and not easily nor gracefully.

And when that great block began to tremble and then tumbled it signalled the end of an era. An era which ushered in gradually profound and far-reaching changes in social awareness and a conception leading to the slow, convoluted birth of the present-day social and national health services.

Although the Manor officially started off life as Derby Union Poor Law Institution it and its predecessor in Osmaston Road were always known as "the workhouse." Much of the grimness associated with those places, so graphically etched by Charles Dickens, had retreated before more enlightened times when, in, July 1877, the Manor's first residents moved in to what was known then as Boundary House. A meal and entertainment to follow, organised by a Mr J. Turner, had been their farewell before filing through the stern portals of the Osmaston Road workhouse. Much of that earlier building survives although greatly altered in parts and to-day houses the Royal Crown Derby works, established there in 1879.

Workhouses as generally perceived were born of the 1834 Poor Law Act. They were large buildings, not necessarily because of a considerable population of poor and destitute, but to accept more inmates when hard times pressed and work became scarce. Summarised, the workhouse's role was to force the able-bodied idle and shiftless into work and provide regular accommodation only for the most incapable and unfortunate. Commonly they were known as "Bastiles," and the Osmaston Road complex, built in 1839, was no exception. However, that soubriquet did not transfer to Boundary House, "the Spike" being preferred.

Should those not inclined to work decide to seek relief then into the workhouse they went. Outdoor relief placed enormous strains on a finite public purse. Forcing the relief seekers to take up residence in a workhouse meant there would be some return. Life inside was hard, food basic, amenities sparse. But, as social historians have pointed out, for the desperately poor and chronically sick anything had to be better than life on the outside. At least those unfortunates ate regularly, were sheltered from the excesses of winter and received basic medical attention. And for the handicapped there was regular care and refuge from a world in which they had no part to play. What people really dreaded about workhouses was the segregation, the grey regimentation and, worst of all in their eyes, the social disgrace. Many were too proud to seek indoor relief, preferring to suffer the far greater degradation of their world outside with its grinding poverty, constant hunger and chronic poor health.

By the 1870s softening of attitudes by the authorities had brought about more relaxed regimes. Changes saw the closing of Osmaston Road workhouse and the opening of Boundary House. Conditions were less cramped, diet more varied and elderly married couples were allowed to live together. The complex could house six hundred and fifty inmates. And, reflecting its increasing medical role, Boundary House contained provision for two-hundred-and-twenty-five infirmary patients.

More improvements, minor but significant in their way, were initiated by the Board of Guardians, such as the well-behaved being permitted a daily newspaper, a ration of tobacco or snuff and well as tea-making facilities. To-day we may think being denied such basic pleasures as something quite extraordinary; that they were is a measure of what life could be like for the less fortunate.

Boundary House's role moved more away from the original workhouse concept with the Local Government Act of 1928, followed in 1930 by the transfer of the Poor Law functions away from the Board of Guardians to the County Borough of Derby. More changes and the workhouse image now just a shadow, although one that no enlightenment would ever quite disperse. Caring for the sick came more to the fore, although accommodation of the poor and destitute remained a prime function. By 1948 Boundary House was under the authority of a hospital management committee and with it the name changed after seventy years to the more familiar Manor Hospital. More changes, with the last of the residents leaving in 1976 to move into purpose-built housing. The hospital's last role was that of a geriatric hospital until final closure in 1988. Time and neglect had taken its toll of a once-fine building and the decision was taken to demolish the entire complex. The Southmead block, a familiar outline to generations of Derby people, came tumbling down early in 1992. For weeks piles of red bricks lay everywhere until carted away, most to be recycled in some Manchester building project.

Working close by the Manor, I took the opportunity before its destruction to search for a reminder of the most well-known resident there when it was still Boundary House. Someone I knew recalled that within the block there had been an elaborately painted ceiling but was unsure as to more precise details. Try as I could, I failed to locate the decoration; maybe it had long since been whitewashed over. Which would have been a shame for on square footage alone the work would have been worth a considerable amount of money, based on the hundreds of pounds, probably thousands now, people are prepared to pay for the small still-life fruit or nature studies painted by the artist.

Last days at "The Manor"

Charles Archer died at Boundary House in 1931 and despite assuring many during his long life that one day he and his paintings would be famous it took more than thirty years after his death before the immodest prediction bore fruit. During the Sixties his meticulous brushwork came to the fore. London dealers were happy to handle his studies of hedgerows and fruit and there were sales at Christie's. Local recognition came with an exhibition in February 1967 at Matlock's Tawney House. Ten years later, at a Derby auction, an Archer still-life reached what was believed to be a record price with a south Yorkshire collector prepared to pay £650 for a painting *circa* 1918.

Archer in his day was a well-known character, but for all that not a great deal is known about the man. Presumably born in Derby since his father kept a shop in London Road, dealing in paintings, engravings and antiques, Charles grew into a giant of man, well over six feet tall, rather handsome and sporting a beard. However, drink proved a problem and many a time a painting fresh off the easel would change hands for the price of a bottle.

This Bohemian character entertained no doubts about his ability and had no hesitation in stopping complete strangers in the street to tell them that when they were dead they would be forgotten, but his paintings would be famous and one day be worth thousands of pounds. At times he enlivened an otherwise dull journey by entertaining passengers on Derby's trams with accounts of his artistic life.

When Charles Archer entered Boundary House is not known, but it came as a result of dropping a heavy hot iron on a leg while re-lining a canvas. The move proved fortuitous for an enlightened Board of Guardians recognised that Archer was right, he was a man of some artistic talent despite an awkward fondness for the bottle. They encouraged him to paint and indeed the years at the workhouse are accepted as probably his most productive. A room high in the Southmead clock tower was his to use as a studio. Archer died at the age of seventy and behind he left as a sign of his gratitude to Boundary House a ceiling painted in his customary elaborate style. Examples of his work can be found here and there, some in Derby's art gallery others in Derby homes; payment, maybe, for an acceptable cure for thirst.

11

A Gin at the Magpie

Should the unwary suddenly come across it they could be excused for thinking they had accidently discovered some medieval torture machinery or maybe a gallows tree sufficient for group hangings. The centre-piece is a large horizontal wheel several feet above the ground. Standing lonesome among fields shaped by familiar grey stone walls and not far from the attractive, seemingly almost deserted village of Sheldon, the dark wooden structure defies explanation. What was its purpose? Who built it? When was it built? All reasonable questions, since there is no patina of time or the elements on the strong timbers. No other similar structure exists anywhere in Derbyshire to give the inquirer a lead.

Yet once there were many of these powerful-looking contraptions and not so many years ago at that. Some as large as this one but generally smaller although performing the same function. Explanations are near to hand for close by stand the impressive ruins of the Magpie lead mine, the sole substantial reminder of an important industry that originated in Roman times, maybe earlier. Amid the ruined site the visitor can discover shaft entrances, the manager's residence, an engine-pumping house of Cornish design, the winding engine shed and lift mechanism and many other, slighter, traces of a once-busy mine.

Had it not been for long, patient toiling by members of the Peak District Mines Historical Society then the Magpie, too, might well have gone the way of the hundreds of others, to become grass-covered lumps and bumps where concrete slabs covered dangerous shafts with surrounding fencing to ward off inquisitive people and cattle. Those same members also built the "gallows tree," which in reality is a beautifully reconstructed gin once powered by horses to haul up to the surface lead ore and detritus from the miles of galleries running hither and thither like arteries many hundreds of feet below.

While lead mines may not share in the glamour of their gold and silver brethren they do draw on the same fund of fanciful names. When Derbyshire's rich deposits were being worked the ore was coming up out of such places as the Wham Engine, Brandy Bottle, Black Marble, Innocent, Silence and Children's Fortune mines. Evocative names that cry out for explanations. What is the reason for Crash Purse, the thinking behind Blobber or Ball Eye mines? The Good Luck workings require no explanation.

Derbyshire's lead industry stretched back nearly two millenia. In the 14th-century its product was being exported to Europe, delivered by an enterprise based on customs shaped by time and laws of sufficient gravity and complexity to require its own courts. Some survive still and one based at the former lead centre of Wirksworth, the Great Barmote Court, is recognised as being the world's oldest industrial court. Nowadays with lead no longer mined its function is virtually ceremonial.

When miners were fully employed, the stealing of lead was regarded as a most serious offence. First and second transgressions were punishable by fines; further offences, up until the early 1850s, demanded more severe measures:

"The third time he commits such a theft
Shall have a knife stuck through his hand to the shaft
Into the stow, and there till death shall stand
Or loose himself by cutting loose his hand."

During the industry's most productive times mines ranged from those owned by the large companies down to the small affairs worked by families and handed down through generations. Conservative estimates place the number of mine shafts in limestone Derbyshire at around seventy thousand.

While not as dangerous as coal mining, another Derbyshire industry, digging out and hauling the ore to the surface was harsh, unhealthy work. Few made more than a bare living, while some family-owned mines were only worked part-time. Daniel Defoe visited Derbyshire during a tour of England and in his fascinating *Tour through England & Wales*, published in 1734, described a miner clambering out from a mine shaft. A "most uncouth spectacle; he was cloathed all in leather, had a cap of the same without brims, some tools in a little basket which he drew up with him . . . " Defoe went on:

> "For his person, he was as lean as a skeleton, pale as a dead corpse, his hair and beard a deep black, and his flesh lank, and as we thought, something of the colour of the lead itself, and being very tall and lean he look'd like an inhabitant of the dark regions below, who had just ascended into the world of light."

Why the Magpie, one of the biggest in its day with a main shaft seven hundred and twenty-eight feet deep, has survived in near-complete form is due to the former extensive wealth of its seams or "rakes." There is a documented history of the remote site reaching back to the 1740s. And a fair share of good times and bad times, the latter because of recession or the common curse of mines, water. Closures came when the galleries flooded, a problem usually overcome by the bringing in of some latest pumping technique. But always the water eventually came back in untold millions of gallons, driving the miners back to the surface and drowning the lead ore. While lead remained the main quarry, towards the end miners were seeking out blende, one of the sulphur ores.

In the last sixty years or so of its long life the Magpie

suffered closure more than once, frustrated by increasing costs, declining markets and, as ever, flooding. Another attempt to get the Magpie operational again came in 1951 when a London-based mining company decided to risk its money. For a few more years the old mine yielded up a harvest but the venture never really found its feet. In the end, inevitably, flooding forced the miners back to the surface and the owners took the decision to shut down, doing so in 1958. The last outpost of a traditional Derbyshire industry going back two thousand years had finally accepted its fate.

Disputes and mining were synonymous. Mine records are full of quarrels placed before the industry's courts for settlement. One of the more serious occurred at the Magpie in 1833, with two rival claims over a lead vein. Bearing in mind the rabbit warren of main and subsidiary galleries stretching out to the veins, the burrowing of centuries, such claims were

Horse-gin, Magpie Mine

inevitable. The dispute at the Magpie turned ugly. One side, in an attempt to force out their rival, ignited sulphur in one of the galleries. Three men perished, their lungs groping for air. Four hundred feet above where the three died stands the reconstructed horse gin, coincidental memorial to a tragedy of greed. Five men were acquitted of murder at the subsequent trial. The three widows placed a curse on the mine and a ghost is reputed to haunt the galleries ever since

While inquiring visitors should find much to interest them above ground, probably the more impressive remains are hidden hundreds of feet below. The mine stands above and a mile from the River Wye and there must have been times when the Magpie's engineers, faced with yet another inundation, thought the ground between one gigantic sponge. Not that the Magpie was unusual, most lead mines suffered flooding and one common solution was the boring of a drainage channel or "sough" (pronounced "suff") as they are known in Derbyshire.

The potential yield from the Magpie was still sufficient for the owners to agree to the construction of a sough of sufficient proportions to solve the flooding menace once and for all. And so the last one ever to be driven in a Derbyshire lead mine was commenced in 1874 and completed in 1881. Cost had originally been estimated at £8,000. However, the engineers met with more problems than anticipated and the owners finished up paying out nearly £35,000.

Something like eight million gallons of water a day still run down the twisting, bending Magpie sough to empty into the Wye. Its exit, or "tail," is quite easily located, again thanks to the dedicated work of the Peak District Mines Historical Society. The proportions of the mile-long tunnel were big enough to permit the use of boats to transport the ore from the mine's galleries rather than laboriously hauling it to the surface. Three locks were installed to control water flow. Early this century the boat in use was a slim craft indeed, measuring twenty-four feet in length and just four feet in the beam.

For all the engineering ingenuity that went into the sough's construction, water continued to flood the Magpie far too often and its failure went a long way in the reaching of that final decision to close down for good.

12

Fall from Grace

Nearly forty years had slipped away before I finally entered through the doors of Kedleston Hall, that majestic residence just north of Derby. When a youngster I cycled past the gates often enough and later enjoyed delightful summer-long days fishing the lake separating Cutler and Markeaton brooks. Behind me lay Robert Adam's masterpiece to delight the eye when the rudd were less inclined to temptation.

Anyway, the time came when I finally paid my entrance fee. Like thousands before me I wandered through the noble rooms and handsome galleries, admired paintings, sculptures and furnishing, much them reflecting the taste of the Curzon family's most illustrious member, the fourth Lord Scarsdale, garnered during his term of office as Viceroy of India around the turn of the century.

What most took my attention was not the great house and its treasures nor the splendid gardens. On my way to those gardens and crossing over a small bridge above an open passageway, I glanced over. There stretched out on the cobbles below was a white marble statue of an elegant young man dressed in what I presumed to be Regency fashion. Closer inspection failed to locate a plaque bearing words of explanation. Neither had the statue fallen off a plinth or just simply toppled over. Whoever carved the curiosity had intended the young man to be portrayed in that recumbent manner.

So why – and what? In the days following, I trawled the shelves of Derby's libraries, pulling out book after book on Derbyshire's stately homes; consulted local guide books, flicked through newspaper and magazine cuttings dealing with Kedleston Hall. But nowhere did I find mention of the fallen man of marble. The lack of reference was quite as puzzling as the monument itself. Then, by chance, I met someone employed at the hall and at last the mystery was solved.

Known as *The Fallen Poet*, the statue had been brought to Kedleston by a daughter of the fourth lord. Presumably not in appreciation of artistic merit but for the intriguing form. The poet and his fall are allegorical, the tumble not a physical thing but a fall from grace. As a poet he had enjoyed fleeting success until exposed and disgraced before society which discovered he had plagiarised the works of others more gifted.

That is what I was told. As an explanation it enjoyed plausibility, so there I let the matter rest.

The Fallen Poet, Kedleston

13

Death of the "Demon Barber"

It seems a contradiction that the man who created the Demon Barber of Fleet Street, murdered Maria Marten on countless occasions and stalked and pounced as The Terror of Epping Forest, should have died peacefully in bed. For that is where Tod Slaughter made his final exit and in Derby. His "Exit stage left" came on 19 February, 1956 while lodging at the Scarsdale Arms in Colyear Street. Tod had just completed a twice-nightly week's run at the Hippodrome Theatre, just along the road. The old pub, said once to have had a music hall attached, was pulled down in 1965. In its place rose the Pennine Hotel, a building of monumental ugliness and a visible argument for not allowing accountants near a drawing board. Once the hotel contained a cinema, of which more later.

Maybe the description "going over the top" was not around when Tod Slaughter trod the boards, but it fitted well his exaggerated method of acting. He would roll his eyes, rant and roar, glide round the stage rubbing his hands in gory anticipation and coined the expression, "I'll soon polish 'im off," for Sweeney Tod the Demon Barber. In short he waded through enough blood, mayhem, gore and bodies to gratify the most blood-thirsty audience. Slaughter was master of his art of Grand Guignol. Jenny Lynn, the wife who outlived him, usually was cast as victim. Raymond Lane, manager of the Hippodrome, on learning of the old actor's death, rightly remarked, "The theatre will be immeasurably poorer. He was king of the old-time melodrama."

The old Hippodrome, Derby

I saw him just once, a few years earlier (I think at the Grand Theatre in Babington Lane) in the role of Spring-heeled Jack, the Terror of Epping Forest. A memorable experience, for that was a play out of time, of a genre almost confined by then to theatre histories. The evening proved enormous fun; hissing the villain, recoiling in horror at his evil deeds, cheering the hero (or heroine). Once you tuned into the style, what followed proved pure entertainment.

The measure of Slaughter's craft was that he kept going, often with considerable success, a form of theatre that really came to end with the 1914-18 war. It belonged to the Victorian age, with its gas lights, dark alleys, horse-drawn cabs rattling over cobbled streets enveloped in fog. The story of Spring-heeled Jack is based on fact, although the villain was not quite so villainous as Tod or the "penny-dreadfuls" portrayed him. Many years later I learned Jack's true identity. A magazine editor was sufficiently moved to accept my article on the Epping Forest menace, only to reject it at the last moment when Jack's descendant turned up and, rightly I suppose, objected. Incidentally research for that article uncovered a centuries-old murder in Paris from which, some claim, grew the legend of the Demon Barber.

The Demon Barber, Jack and the slayer of Maria Marten: they were the three roles on which Slaughter founded his reputation. He claimed to have played the Barber over four thousand times, and made the most of it. Should there be a public house near the theatre, it would not be unknown for him, dressed in the part – bloody hands and bloodied barber's apron – to nip out for a quick drink to the consternation of the bar customers. The Barber's victims were chopped up into pieces small enough fill meat pies, baked by Mrs Lovett next door; Tod made it his business to have fresh hot pies on sale during the interval. All in the cause of verisimilitude.

Tod Slaughter, a Geordie born Norman Carter Slaughter, was seventy years old when he arrived at a bitterly cold Derby in 1956 to play in what would be his last production, the grisly slaying of Maria Marten in the infamous red barn at Polstead in Suffolk. For the final time of countless times he played William Corder, seducer and then murderer of the mole-catcher's daughter. But this was not full production, just extracts in a week given over to the good old days of the English music hall. In a rather dismissive review the *Derby Evening Telegraph's* critic thought the production one "which will entertain those who have a nostalgic feeling for the good old days . . . to others it may seem dull and boring." A sad note for the final appearance of a great theatrical, a man who of himself many thought a legend.

At the end of the week's run Tod Slaughter made his was to Colyear Street and the Scarsdale Arms, for his last curtain. Next day, a Sunday, the landlord's nine-year old son discovered the old actor dead in his bed.

His story does not quite end there. As already mentioned, the Pennine Hotel grew on the site of the public house. When completed in 1966 part of the building was used as a cinema, first the Superama and then renamed the Odeon Pennine. During its ten years as a cinema there were occasional reports from staff members of a wraith-like figure seen gliding about when the place was closed. A ghost glimpsed only briefly and with no aura of menace. For some reason the staff named him Fred.

In 1976 the cinema closed and re-opened as a disco. With that change of role Fred displayed a preference for music and disappeared for good. Some years later someone learning of the former cinema's ghost recalled that it haunted the site of the old Scarsdale Arms and drew the obvious conclusion that the spectre must have been none other than the man who created the demonic Sweeney Todd, Tod Slaughter.

One must wonder if the ghost ever wished he had his trusty old cut-throat razor about him and muttering, "I'll soon polish 'im off," sought to polish off whoever insultingly nicknamed him "Fred."

14

"And what am I offered?"

Selling one's spouse could only be viewed as an abhorrent act but there must be many a husband who, reaching for the wilder shores of fantasy, has not indulged himself. And no doubt there are wives who on occasions might devoutly yearn for the same facility. And yet in fact it is little more than a century since what is accepted as the last recorded sale took place at Sheffield in 1887, with the husband being quite happy to pocket five shillings on the deal.

The trade in wives had declined steadily throughout the nineteenth century. Newspapers were able to report them only occasionally, which might lead the curious to think it had been a somewhat isolated business anyway. But was it? There is nothing to indicate when the selling of men's better halves first started, when it reached its peak – and what sort of numbers are we talking about, anyway?

There is the argument that newspapers did report sales because it was a quite ancient business much in decline and, conversely, attracting attention. From such an argument it follows surely that once these transactions had been relatively widespread and so hardly worth devoting newsprint to. Such could be the case, for what few reports are available usually provide little more than the barest details and so, perhaps inadvertently, underlined the antiquity of the custom. And if, as some have claimed, such auctions go back to Viking times, then there were no newspapers to report them and what chroniclers were about had more momentous happenings to record than the doings of the poorer classes among which these deals took place. Others claim that wife-selling goes back even further, seeing possible origins in Anglo-Saxon times. Then the law provided that should the wife of a freeman be seduced by another freeman then that man was obliged to pay what was known as his full *weregeld* and purchase another wife for the injured husband and deliver that purchase to his door. The subsequent fate of the seduced is not revealed.

Derbyshire has several sales on record, their ritual much in keeping with those in other parts. Market towns were the usual venues with the auctions being conducted around the market cross or similar prominent feature. Some were known as Horn Markets but why is unclear, as is so much about these exchanges. More certain is the accompanying ceremonial. The husband, having first paid a beast sale toll, would enter the market place leading his wife by a rope halter tied around her neck. Two or three times she would be led round the market-place and finally tied to the market cross or some other handy pillar. Or maybe confined within a sheep pen or secured to railings. Nothing else quite so much indicates the then lowly regard for women as those debasing rituals, nothing but parallels of cattle marts.

Following the ringing of a hand-bell to draw a crowd the sale began, the husband bawling out that his wife could be purchased and all reasonable offers would be considered. Not that it was essential that he conduct proceedings, a market official or Poor Law officer might be persuaded. At Swadlincote in February 1790 an absconding husband left his wife as a charge on the parish, and she was eventually sold off by a parish official.

Once a bid had been accepted, bills of sale and any other necessary documents were drawn up to the satisfaction of both parties. Then once again the wife was obliged to parade

Wirksworth market-place

around the market-place, still controlled by the halter but led now by her purchaser.

Public houses were popular alternative venues, again sales concluding with the signing of papers which, as far as the participants were concerned, enjoyed the same authority as properly drawn-up legal papers. Sometimes lawyers were asked to handle the paper work. An Ashbourne lawyer was approached in May 1739 to draw up articles of sale after Thomas Frost of Kirk Ireton auctioned off not only his wife but their five children as well, to Joseph Handford, a clog maker of the village. Pleading integrity, the lawyer declined but in doing so suggested another who might not be too particular. This individual obliged and the "delivery of the goods" documentation was duly completed to the satisfaction of all concerned.

Derbyshire's best-known auction took place in April 1773 when William Bradley, a mason by trade, turned up at Wirksworth market-place leading his wife, Anne, by the customary halter. George Ward was the purchaser and happy to pay the rather handsome sum of two guineas together with a silver watch. Formalities completed, Mr Ward went off with his acquisition. As for Bradley, he hurried off to the local newspaper office to insert a notice to the effect that he would not be responsible for any debt that Anne Bradley (or Ward) might contract in his or her name. Furthermore, "all persons are cautioned against giving her, the said Anne Bradley, any credit on the account of her much injured husband."

Alfreton hosted several sales, including what may have been Derbyshire's last. One Saturday night in 1882 at a public house, in a room full of men, a young husband sold his wife for the price of a pint of beer. For her part she removed her wedding ring and "from that time considered herself the property of the purchaser." However, this rather sad barter with its absence of former ritual might more properly be regarded as an abuse, the final throes of an old custom. Or maybe just a sordid incident posing under the guise of a ritual which, despite social disapproval, had nevertheless once been held as serious and binding among the poorer classes.

At Chapel-en-le-Frith in 1802 a wife and child, together with "a great quantity of furniture," went up for sale at the Market Cross and the lot was knocked down for eleven shillings. An observer commented there was enough furniture "to set up a beggar." Values on wives varied wildly. In Derby the previous year a Langley farmer, one Thomas Bott, parted with his spouse for just one shilling and sixpence.

Belper market-place served as the arena in August 1873 for a wife who, as a local reporter ungallantly noted, "was the interesting article submitted to competition." What makes this incident even more unusual was her insistence on being offered for sale. Her husband, a man named Thompson, had decided to emigrate to America, wearied of his wife and her preference to accumulate debt rather than cultivate thrift. When his worldly goods were displayed for auction, Mrs Thompson marched in on the proceedings to stridently stake a claim to part of the proceeds. Either that, she warned, or the auctioneer must sell her, too.

Matters did not quite work out the way Mrs Thompson anticipated. The auctioneer refused her ultimatum but from the crowd stepped a man who offered to conduct the proceedings. Quickly the essential rope halter was fashioned and the "interesting article" ceremoniously led off to the market-place. But no bids were forthcoming. There may have been those who knew why Mr Thompsom had absented himself from Belper and were not prepared to risk a similar departure. How the affair ended is not recorded, beyond the report's publisher regretting that the "indignant nailers" of Belper did not accommodate the man who had led Mrs Thompson by a halter with "a dozen well laid on with the rope's end."

Apart from very occasional reports from other parts of the country of husbands being charged and sentenced to a few weeks' hard labour for offering their wives up, the law did not unduly bother itself with these auctions, as is evidenced by an account of an incident in Ashbourne from a rather unexpected source.

Major General Pillet of the French Army had the misfortune to be captured during the Napoleonic Wars and subsequently arrived in England as a prisoner of war. There were several centres where such prisoners were billeted, Ashbourne being one of them. Pillet took the opportunity permitted by parole of honour to travel about England. He recorded much of what he saw and later, hostilities over and back home in France, published his experiences.

Presumably this senior officer had to report in somewhere during his wanderings, which would explain his arrival in Ashbourne where some one hundred and seventy fellow officers were kept prisoner, not altogether disagreeably. While in the town he witnessed a wife being auctioned in the market-place. Not quite believing what he saw, Pillet questioned a magistrate, there to keep an eye on proceedings. He informed the major general of his doubts if there existed any rights to forbid the sale. As far as the magistrate was concerned the sale rested "on a custom preserved by the people of which perhaps it would be dangerous to deprive them by any law for that purpose." Pillet discovered that the sale had the consent of the wife, as was necessary, and that generally such sales followed on a wife's perceived misconduct. Writing in the idiom of the auction room, Pillet recorded that the buyer "is generally a lover of the commodity sold, and is well-acquainted with it." Moreover, being brought to the market-place and paraded served merely "for the sake of form." At Ashbourne, according to the Frenchman, there had been an attempt by a Justice of the Peace to prevent this particular sale but the town's constables had wisely retired after being jostled and pelted by the crowd.

Closer examination of admittedly limited evidence shows that these wife-sales were not quite the free and easy affairs as might be inferred. No sale could ever take place without the wife's consent; to proceed otherwise would certainly have stirred local magistrates into action. Nor are there any known reports of more than one person ever bidding for a switch of favours. All indications are that the buyer had been accepted by those involved (as suggested by Pillet) before the procession to the market-place or the haggling in some public house.

These extraordinary auctions dwelt very much in the province of the poor and were without a doubt a rough and ready form of divorce in an age where divorce, if obtainable, remained only in reach of the influential and wealthy. Having said that, there are accounts of gentlemen purchasing wives and at least one nobleman, but these were very much the exception. There are rare cases, with only two or three on record, where wives sold husbands; none in Derbyshire. Apart from newspaper condemnation, the authorities took little prohibitive action other than nominal. The occasional sentence to a short term of hard labour satisfied the Law.

On the other side of the fence there had been some laxity over the conduct of marriages. So much so that during the reign of George III (1760-1820) the authorities became considerably alarmed at the rising incidence of wedding ceremonies in private houses and taverns, often attended by dubious ritual and at times without witnesses. As a result a law was passed banning marriages in such places and was not relaxed until the 1830s when, for the first time, they were permitted to be conducted in non-Anglican churches and register offices.

No matter what public ritual may have suggested, wife-selling transactions were taken most seriously and bills of sale as highly regarded as any marriage certificate. That is if marriage certificates were ever involved. Common law unions were more the order of the day among the poorer classes than is generally realised. Neither the Law nor the Church bothered themselves too much. Both tolerated the ways and customs of the lower classes, provided they did not offend public decency too much. Church-going did not play a prominent, or often even a minor role, in the common round or the trivial tasks of the poor. And provided nothing occurred to frighten the horses, church ministers contented themselves with more conventional and socially acceptable congregations.

15

Black Jack, Bleu Jaune . . . ?

Here ranging through her
vaulted ways
On Nature's alchemy
You gaze
See how she forms the gem,
The ore
And all her magazines galore

So some unknown versifier recorded his feelings on seeing Derbyshire's extraordinary gemstone, one of the world's rarest, in its natural setting. Like so many he, too, had marvelled at the fragile stone with its erratic bands of blues, purples, white and occasional reds, mined out of Mam Tor hill at Castleton in north Derbyshire. Mines, usually extensions of natural caves, delve into the Tor, the only known source anywhere of this peculiar caste of calcium fluoride. The beautiful banding and contrasting colours of Blue John, as the semi-precious stone is called, comes from the iron and oil traces found in Mam Tor, the top of which also contains rock-seeping oil. Nature's convulsions when the world was young did the rest.

Guide books, local histories, tourist pamphlets, state that the Romans, searching for lead and anything else, were the first to discover and then exploit the stone. They had built a camp, Anavio, close by the present-day village of Brough. As their empire expanded through the Middle East and into Europe they sent back to Rome the finest marbles, precious stones and crystals to adorn their capital and the elegant villas of leading citizens. They thought that Blue John was worthy of the effort. It is reported (not least in auction room brochures) that two vases born of the stone were recovered from the ash-covered ruins of Pompeii. Pliny described a particular piece, the vasa *Murrhina*, recognised by some as Blue John: "Its colours were purple and white in undulating bands and usually separated by a third band in which the two colours, being mixed, assumed the tint of flame."

That infamous dilettante and well-known murderer, the Emperor Nero, also found Derbyshire's rare stone to his avaricious taste. Very much so if tales that he drank blood from a Blue John goblet were correct. On another rumoured occasion he paid 6,000 *sestertia* (£120,000 in modern terms) for a bowl. Another highly desirable artefact valued at 300 *talents* (£70,000) belonged to Petronius. Unfortunately for him Nero took the notion it would display better in his collection and so, being emperor and could do no wrong, had its owner condemned to death on some pretext so he could get his blood-stained hands on it. Petronius, learning of his fate, dashed the Blue John to the floor. A fragile mineral, it shattered into a hundred pieces.

Curiously, the exploitation of Blue John seems to have ceased rather abruptly after the Romans withdrew from Britain in 407AD. For well over a thousand years absolutely nothing is heard of the gemstone, neither in records nor, more significantly, as artefacts. However the remote Man Tor region had not been forgotten. The Romans certainly had discovered lead and that mineral continued being sought after down succeeding centuries. And traces of that industry are easily found, the most notable being the Speedwell cavern mine part way up the craggy Winnats Pass. Going towards

Mam Tor itself the long-abandoned Odin mine is another prominent site, complete with its gritstone wheel ore-crushing circle.

Mam Tor and Odin Mine

There were people who saw the caves and caverns dotted around not only as a source of minerals but places to live. Most accommodating was the enormous Peak Cavern where, just within its yawning entrance, not only did they build their houses but founded a rope works which continued in production to within living memory.

Charles Cotton, in 1682, wrote of those near-troglodytes:

Houses and Barns for Men and Beasts behoof
With walls distinct under one solid roof.
Stacks of both hay and turf, which yields a scent
Can only come from Satan's fundament.

Forty years later Blue John was re-discovered (or discovered?) and an industry born. At its height sixteen mines burrowed into Mam Tor. Workshops to cut and form the raw mineral were to be found not only in Castleton but also the Matlocks, Buxton and Ashford-in-the-Water. The gemstone's appeal had been immediate. From 1770 to 1840 craftsman drew on their skills to fashion ornaments and jewellery from the subtly coloured and so-delicate stone. Their products became a fashionable necessity in the drawing rooms of 18th-century grand houses.

Of all those who created such beautiful things, no one's work was so much sought after as Matthew Boulton's. An enterprising Birmingham engineer with a famous factory at Soho, he is now more remembered for his partnership with James Watt in developing steam engines to power factory machines. However, he was also one of the most celebrated silversmiths of his day and it was his business acumen as well as skill in working the Derbyshire gemstone that turned it into a world-wide fashion.

Matthew Boulton could rightly be regarded as the father of the Blue John industry; the magnificent *objects d'art* he created in his workshops bear testimony to the passion he bore the rare stone. He further excelled as a salesman. And there are those who see in that artful ability the origins of Blue John's "Roman connection" and claim he promoted the belief as a means of promoting his wares. In support is the fact that Boulton was by no means ignorant of Roman history nor its artefacts. Such ploys are not unknown. A humorous parallel is the famous Willow Pattern porcelain which many presume is the depicting of an ancient Chinese story of doomed love. In fact it dates no further back than 1780 when a Thomas Turner of Caughley in The Potteries launched both the design and the tale. A party of Chinese some years ago visited the area and were enchanted by the story. They had never heard it before.

A telling point against Roman origins is that the fine, delicate working of Blue John became possible only after the discovery during the early days of the new industry that the brittle stone gained in strength from being boiled in resin. The process also added a most attractive yellow shade, a colour not mentioned by Pliny in his description of the vasa *Murrhina.*

Business boomed for Boulton but he was obliged to pay a hefty price for the raw material. He resolved to purchase an interest in a Blue John mine and wrote to a friend in Derby, the influential Dr. Erasmus Darwin, to enlist his aid. " . . . but above all I beg you will be quite secret as to my intentions, and never let M. Boulton and John Blue be named in the same sentence." Unfortunately for the Birmingham engineer, his soliciting bore no fruit.

Demand kept the Castleton mines busy with the result that by 1829 the mineral was becoming noticeably scarcer and craftsmen were having to pay up to £40 a ton. Then the public began to lose their taste for this strange product of Nature's studio and the industry began to decline. Mines closed and by the Great War the beautifully banded stone was being used as a flux in the manufacture of steel and chemicals

In recent years Blue John has deservedly recaptured some of its former glory. However, the source of the raw material continues to dwindle; no other deposits have ever been discovered. Where sixteen mines once probed for the unique mineral only the Blue John and Treak mines remain operational. Notwithstanding, anyone who visits the Mam Tor caves and mines to-day will testify that they still have an important role to play in the local economy, as tourist showplaces. Castleton itself is probably benefiting more than it ever did. The unique gemstone is almost secondary to the caves themselves but the colours, together with the weird shapes of age-defying stalactites and stalagmites and fancy-named caverns, most cunningly illuminated, only serve to emphasise in what a marvellous setting Nature placed this oddity.

The days of shaping Blue John into vases, bodies for clocks, table tops and cups are in the past; they absorb too much of the finite raw material. Once the source dries up then prices have to rise. Not that to-day to obtain a large piece of the carved stone is an inexpensive undertaking. A thirty-inch malachite table top would command around £500 at an auction. Fashioned in Blue John the serious bidder must be prepared to part with something like £8,000. Goblets from the last century fetch in the region of £5,000. Definitely not for sale would be the *tazza* (cup) owned by the Duke of Devonshire and kept at Chatsworth House and said to be the largest piece ever cut from a single raw piece, in this case an eighteen-inch cube. For the modest purse the specialist shops around Castleton, Bakewell and Matlock will repay the careful shopper.

Severely frowned upon is searching on the ground for natural samples, however small. Blue John, like wild flowers, is a protected item. As a young lad learning the joys of hiking I would scratch through the small piles of detritus to be found up in the Winnats Pass and on Mam Tor's steep slopes and take home some of the larger stones. They formed part of my personal memorabilia; alas, like my youth, they are gone

And why Blue John? No one is quite certain. Some claim it comes from the French for blue and yellow *Bleu Jaune*, a reminder of the French clockmakers who incorporated the mineral in their intricate timepieces. Others say it is a simple, humorous twist on "Black Jack," bestowed by John Kirk and Joseph Hall, two miners more accustomed to digging for a marble of that name.

16

"According to Custom"

I cannot bear the gaze of men, and live in constant fear
That chance once more will bare my back, where stripes
do yet appear.
Not deep, nor livid, starting scars, distinguishing the brave,
But sickly, faint, and ghostly things, like shadows on a grave.

(Song of a Soldier)

For three-quarters of an hour Chesterfield's market-place echoed to the hypnotic *rat-a-tat-tat* as the regimental drummer beat out the call to arms. And for the same time Chesterfield Militia's armed volunteers remained aloof to the call. Not one reported for duty. They took their cue from their adjutant and his fellow officers who gazed impassively on the scene. Alongside the town's citizens had also assembled to watch the brutal flogging of a soldier, a drummer, of the 2nd Nottinghamshire Regiment. A court-martial had sentenced him to an appointment with the dreaded cat o'nine tails for striking a sergeant during the execution of his duty.

Striking a superior officer was and remains a most serious offence in the military world and the unknown drummer probably drew a sentence of five hundred lashes. Soldiers had died under the assault of fewer. Flogging was the principal method of instilling and maintaining discipline; one hundred strokes was considered a light sentence. Some endured a thousand (virtually a death sentence) and the team of drummers or farriers detailed to inflict that punishment needed nearly *four hours* to carry it out. King George III thought a sentence to fifteen hundred strokes somewhat excessive and suggested, murder apart, a thousand "sufficient" for breaches of discipline.

While the British Army's record in the field is a magnificent one, as many a regimental museum testifies, the glory largely reflects on its officers. In the 18th and 19th-centuries the soldiers themselves, although essential, were little regarded. The Duke of Wellington despised them, observing that they were "taken from the lowest orders of society." As far as he and the majority of his colleagues were concerned, that is where they would stay. Said the Iron Duke, "They are the very worst members of society – the scum of the earth, enlisted for drink. They are all enlisted for drink." Wellington opposed any move for abatement of punishment by flogging and flatly refused to countenance any suggestion of actually abolishing it.

The Duke's finest hour was Waterloo and at that momentous occasion, even as the enemy advanced, there were soldiers being scratched by the cat. Punished, backs lacerated and bloody, they then went on to fight the foe for the glory of England. No Byron to record their doings on the eve of Waterloo. No beauty, no chivalry; just drink, the threat of a whipping and a chance to die. So entrenched the belief that only the cat o'nine tails could keep society's scum in line that Queen Victoria herself commented Parliament had acted "so unwisely" when, in 1881, it abolished flogging in the last army in Europe to use it.

The regard that the majority officers held for the rank and file under their command was by and large reflected by the public in general. By "going for a soldier" a man cut himself off from a society that, except for war-time, would have little time for him. Kipling understood the ordinary fighting man well and knew his bitterest thoughts:

For it's Tommy this, an Tommy that, an'
"Chuck him out, the brute!"
But it's "Saviour of 'is country" when the
guns begin to shoot.

When the flogging of the drummer took place at Chesterfield market-place the regiment would have been billeted out in lodgings or public houses; barracks were a relatively new concept. And if England had not been at war with Napoleon the rank and file would have received "paying out" money from those on whom they were billeted, to go and find some place else.

Despite this disregard, there grew among the ordinary people an abhorrence of how soldiers were treated. Particularly they detested to see or hear soldiers being flogged and from these people sprang the movement that eventually finished flogging in the army. The savaging of that unfortunate drummer resulted in one of the earlier manifestations of that resentment.

Military beatings were encased in grim ritual. The 2nd Nottinghamshire Regiment were paraded under arms and in full dress on 2 July 1805 to watch their comrade's humiliation. The unfortunate drummer would have been bound tightly to three halberds lashed together to form a triangle. Nearby the officers would have loosely assembled, displaying that apathy or indifference so fashionable among their kind. In front of the parade the adjutant read out the court-martial's sentence. Formalities proceeded with the commanding officer, Major George MacGregor, giving his permission to "Carry on".

A small team of drummers carried out the flogging, under the command of an NCO whose duty it was to call out a rythmic "*one*" .. "*two*" .. "*three* . . . As the cat carved its bloody paths over on the drummer's bared back there were those in the ranks unable to stand the sickening sight and fainted. Each blow had to be recorded in a special notebook and when the wretched business was completed, or if Major MacGregor ordered an early release, the entries would be completed with the note that the sentence had been carried out "according to custom."

A normal regimental public flogging, but one at which the watching townspeople became increasingly incensed. As the drummer suffered some in the crowd began pelting the troops with stones and anything else that came to hand. Others called on the soldiers to shoot their officers. After the whipping and the parade dismissed to quarters the crowd remained, their anger rising and hovering on the warm evening air.

Major MacGregor, accompanied by his officers, returned to his quarters. Behind followed a mob several hundred strong shouting abuse and threats. Once the officers were indoors the crowd grew more furious and pelted the building with missiles for half an hour. One person was injured, an elderly servant woman in the major's lodgings, struck by a stone.

Relief came in the form of the Mayor of Chesterfield, Mr. Elam, who assumed responsibility for the situation when Major MacGregor placed the 2nd Nottinghamshire Regiment at his disposal. The Mayor decided to assemble the Chesterfield Militia and ordered that a drummer beat out the call to arms, with the result already described. An ugly impasse had arisen: a crowd in an angry mood, an armed militia refusing to obey the call to arms, a lacerated soldier lying in agony on his blood-soaked bed and a regular regiment close to hand. Mr Elam, showing why he had been elected mayor, gradually took the initiative, slowed down the pace and eventually succeeded in getting part of the crowd to move off. Some spectators refused to be persuaded and when the 2nd Regiment's officers went to assemble their men they had to encounter another barrage of insults and missiles. One of the crowd, Joshua Batty a local shoemaker, appeared to be the leader. Later he was indicted for riot and assault and remanded for an appearance at Derby Assizes. Batty's eventual fate is not known. There were no further incidents in the market-place. A few days later the 2nd Regiment quit Chesterfield and marched over the hills to Ashbourne.

While never attaining the brutality of military flogging, the cat o'nine tails was a common enough punishment within the civilian populace. Applied equally to men and woman, and occasionally children, the whipping usually went little further than a minor bloodying of the exposed back. The crimes that were rewarded by the lash were numerous and, by present day standards, often remarkably trivial.

Chesterfield's market-place must have been a favoured place for carrying out floggings. Alice Pearson was sent there for her punishment in September 1738. Found guilty of stealing some clothing, the judge, displaying what to-day might be termed parochial racial tendencies, commented: "She is a Yorkshire woman. I hope she will be severely punished and sent home."

Chesterfield's last recorded public flogging took place on 4 April 1829. Two men, Henry Scott and John Gee, had been found guilty at Derby Assizes of stealing an ass and they too endured their punishment at the market-place. And, as with that unknown drummer many years before, the sordid event was not well-received by the watching crowd. The animal the pair had stolen, along with horses and donkeys, was protected by law against brutal treatment. Ironically, to steal let alone abuse one, an offender would receive a punishment about as brutal as could be inflicted on any living being.

Punishment by whipping remained law in this country far longer than might be supposed. Military floggings were abolished in 1881. Thirty-three years later the 1914 Criminal Justice Act laid down that no one was to be whipped more than once for one offence and whippings were only permissible in law if the particular offence carried such a sentence. In the 1930s, men found guilty in Manchester of living off immoral earnings were taken on one side and flogged. The 1948 Criminal Justice Act abolished whipping as a court sentence. However, the punishment remained on the books for those found guilty of causing a mutiny in a prison or assaulting prison staff. The Act of 1967 put an end to that last remnant of barbarism.

17

The Gibbet and The Gallows

If crime demands it, let the offender die,
But let no more the Gibbet brave the sky:
No more let vengeance on the dead be hurl'd,
But hide the victim from a gazing world.

Those lines written by the "Minstrel of the Peak," William Newton of Tideswell, are taken from a long, melodramatic poem. Such was its impact on the public and Parliament that a few years later the law was amended to forbid the later gibbeting of criminals who had been sentenced to death by hanging. A gentle and compassionate man, Newton had been moved to write the poem after the gibbeting of a fellow townsman, Anthony Lingard. His brutal slaying of Mrs Hannah Oliver on New Year's Day, 1815, would now be almost forgotten had he not been the last person in England whose corpse would suffer the sordid judicial sentence of being fastened in chains and then suspended in an iron cage, to be butchered by the elements and provide carrion for the birds.

Lingard was lucky. Had his sordid crime been committed some years earlier he would have been still a living thing when encased in the gibbet cage and stayed there until dead; then his cleaned and bleached bones were permitted to remain as a deterrent to others. That gibbeting nor the more merciful hanging failed utterly to deter criminals, and there were many crimes one could swing for, went unheeded by the judiciary. In the end two Derbyshire gibbetings brought about the cessation of such a barbaric practice throughout the kingdom.

Sometime in the 17th-century a tramp called to a thatched cottage near Baslow and begged for food from the old woman living there. She replied there was nothing for idlers the like of him. Unfortunately for her she was cooking bacon and the tramp, infuriated by the answer, seized the pot of boiling fat and despite the woman's struggles forced the liquid down her protesting throat. She scalded to death. Arrested and brought to court the tramp was sentenced to be gibbeted alive and suspended from a wooden post fashioned like a gallows tree close by the scene of his crime. High behind Chatsworth House, home of the Devonshire family, lies bleak Gibbet Moor so named because it was there the murderer starved to death. For days his cries and screams rent the air and, it is said, so distracted the Earl of Devonshire that the nobleman took steps that no more would criminals die in such dreadful fashion.

Hunger sent that unknown killer to the gibbet; greed sent Lingard's body to rot in chains at Wardlow Mires, just north of Wardlow village. A young man of twenty-one he had visited Mrs Hannah Oliver, the keeper at the Mires toll house, in an attempt to persuade her to part with a new pair of red shoes. Lingard, rumoured to have had a liaison with Mrs Oliver, told her he wanted them for a girl friend back in Tideswell. Mrs Oliver refused and a violent quarrel erupted; blows were struck and the toll-keeper died. Her murderer returned to Tideswell and tucked under his arm were the coveted shoes. When Mrs Oliver's coffin went to the graveyard Lingard watched it pass by as he stood drinking in the doorway of a public house.

The murder was soon discovered and an investigation ordered. Lingard came under suspicion, strong enough for him to be arrested and sent to Derby Assizes for trial.

Principal prosecution witness was Samuel Marsden, a Stoney Middleton shoemaker who positively identified the red shoes as a pair he had made for the deceased and had been discovered in Lingard's home. The young killer from Tideswell was hanged in Derby and a party of soldiers accompanied the corpse back for gibbeting, not too far from the toll-house.

Wardlow elected to make the occasion something to remember. Lingard's body gently swung to and fro in its cage, obscenely presiding over the gaiety. In the field below pedlars and travelling tinkers erected their stalls. Trade boomed in the carnival atmosphere. Among the milling crowd strolled William Newton. He found the scene so revolting that it haunted his memory and some time later committed his thoughts in his most famous and highly effective poem, *The Supposed Soliloquy of a Father, Under the Gibbet of his Son, upon one of the Peak Mountains near Wardlow.* How long the corpse remained suspended is uncertain but evidence suggests some considerable time. Certainly until the corpse had been reduced to its skeleton. Years later a Thomas Platt recalled that when a boy he learned that a "cow doctor" from Tideswell had assisted a medical man from Wheaton Hall to take down Lingard's bleached bones. The skull was despatched to Belle Vue in Manchester, to be placed on public display.

Probably the removal took place after 1819, for early in that year the gibbet could still be seen. And maybe familiarly half-noticed by sixteen-years-old Hannah Bocking from nearby Litton. On 22 March she suffered public hanging in Derby for giving a poisoned sweetcake to Jane Grant, also of Litton. The pair had been told to fetch some cows from the field close to where Litton's body had twisted and turned. Hannah's motive for the callous murder is not known. However, it is unlikely she suffered gibbeting; few women did for sensitive authority considered it unbecoming of female modesty since their clothes would also rot along with their bodies.

Gibbeting was abolished in 1834, principally in response

to the outcry stirred up by Newton's tragic poem. None of the gibbet posts have survived in Derbyshire. A reputed site can be visited on a country lane between Lea and Dethick where an old mill stone is pointed out as the base of a gibbet post, but supporting evidence is lacking. There were at least two sites in Derby, one believed to be near the southern corner of Loudon Street and Normanton Road while a gibbet certainly stood somewhere within the area now covered by the Derbyshire Royal Infirmary.

Public hanging survived the gibbet by some years. They too drew large crowds and the whole ghastly ceremonial would be accompanied by fairs, speeches from the gallows tree and a brisk sale in "confessions" dictated by the victim during his last hours in the condemned cell. Dr Johnson, a humane and understanding man otherwise, thoroughly approved of such executions, considering that the "public was gratified by a procession and the criminal supported by it."

Once upon a time Heage village, overlooking the Derwent valley, enjoyed a reputation for its public hangings, or at least providing fodder for the hangman's noose, and noted in the saying, "Heage, where they hang 'em in bunches." A "Heage wash," according to a contemporary preacher, was a euphemism for a hanging. The "bunches" comment probably stems from the hanging for murder of three Heage men, Samuel Bonsall, William Bland and John Hulme, whose collective execution in front of Derby gaol in September, 1842, drew an enormous crowd estimated at fifty thousand. Some spectators were obliged to climb up on nearby buildings to obtain a better view.

There is a misconception that the last public hanging in Derby took place in Agard Street. But it was in that street, at Court No. 4, in February 1862 that widower Richard Thorley murdered Eliza Morrow, a somewhat flighty young mill girl with whom he had been "keeping company." For his grievous sin Thorley danced into eternity at the end of hangman Calcraft's rope on 11 April watched by several thousand

The old Derby gaol

outside the gaol in Vernon Street, the imposing grey stone curtain walls of which dominate the area still.

Thorley, after several days of heavy drinking and brooding over Eliza's preference for the company of a soldier, called to the mean little house in Agard Street and with a razor ended her life. His execution, by the new "drop" method was quick and later his body was removed to within the gaol walls and, with minimum ceremony, quietly buried. According to reports in the *Derby Mercury*, "he died penitent," which is hardly surprising when learning how many religious tracts and sermons he had been subjected to while sitting out his time in the condemned cell.

A growing revulsion over executions being conducted where anyone could witness them was reflected by reports in the *Mercury*. The mood was for reform and decency. And the demeanour of the crowd at Thorley's hanging drew sharp editorial comment, noting that such exhibitions were still popular with certain sections of the public to which "many had walked to till they were foot-sore to secure a sight of the sickening spectacle." There were those who, to observe more closely Calcraft exercising his ghastly trade and ending Lingard's life, had hired telescopes from opticians.

Parliament eventually decreed that executions were to be removed from the public gaze and carried out in a special room behind high prison walls. In 1965 capital punishment was finally abolished; curiously in the last thirty years there have been no less than fifteen attempts to revive a ritual that at its busiest and most public entertained untold thousands.

18

A Rabbi Fleet of Foot

How he came by his curious nickname of "Rabbi" is uncertain. I first heard it far too many years ago when working as an evening newspaper's correspondent in the east Derbyshire town of Heanor, at a time when its connections with the coal fields were still much in evidence. Someone told me that once there had been a famous runner in the town who had beaten all opposition, amateur or professional, that ever challenged him. Parochial pride is permitted exaggeration. Edward Stainesby he was called and there are families of that name, usually with the "e" omitted, still in living in the area.

Although thought of as a Heanor man there is some mystery as to his place of birth as there is about his curious nickname. That he was born on 11 January, 1825, is generally accepted, but the place may well have been Derby. When and where he died remains a puzzle; he can be traced to 1866.

What is certain is that by the age of twenty "Rabbi" Stainesby cut a fine sporting figure of a man. Well-built and muscular, standing over six feet, those who knew him thought him "rather good-looking and attractive." A popular man who enjoyed company and possessed a broad sense of humour that appealed to his listeners. What placed "Rabbi" apart was his natural athletic ability. Had he not that then his life would not have been noteworthy at all; unless one marvels at the variety of work he undertook. He started of earning as a framework-knitter, went on to the trade of lace-maker, labourer, navvy, greengrocer, collier, and became a mobile fishmonger, bringing fish, shrimps, mussels, oysters and crabs to the housewives of Heanor. In his later years, after finishing a shift down the pit, "Rabbi" would go home, hitch up his pony to a cart and, his wife alongside, set off selling salt.

Nature had been kind to "Rabbi" Stainesby. For such a big man he could run remarkably quick, usually competing in mile races. That he had such a talent seemingly did not become apparent until he was nineteen and turned up as a spectator to a race, with cash as prizes. A good-natured individual, he volunteered to hold the clothes of one of the competitors and stood a few yards down the course to watch the race. At the signal to start "Rabbi" decided to run alongside the competitors and, despite being dressed in working clothes and carrying another's, he finished ahead of a professional field.

In a day when professional races were enormously popular in east Derbyshire towns and villages "Rabbi's" course was clear. He went into training and won his first money on Plough Monday, 1845. Once England abounded with special days, most long since discarded following the rise of industrialisation. Anyway, Plough Monday fell on the first Monday after Twelfth Night (a working knowledge of moveable feasts must have been essential in those times) and marked the day when men returned to the plough or daily work. In the country districts farm labourers would pull a plough from door to door to raise money to finance one last round of merry-making.

"Rabbi" observed the day by winning, although there had been some dispute and the judges called upon to settle matters. After that nothing could stop young Stainesby winning a further dozen races in the same year and usually against the best. While not enough is known of this athlete (he also excelled at hurdles and vaulting) the suggestion is

RABBI

THE NOTED FOOT RACER

OF HEANOR.

that in his professional career he consistently carried off prize money, although he never repeated the magic of 1845.

He would enter anything where he could put his athletic bent to the test, putting down his name down for pony and donkey races, even wheelbarrow events. At the Heanor races of 1864 "Rabbi", his glory days as a runner behind him, won a pound on his donkey, Jenny Lind. Later at the same meeting he and Jenny raced again, this time against Raynor, the Heanor chimney sweep, mounted on Lord Byron's Devil. Hundreds watched and saw Raynor struggle while "Rabbi" moved away quite untroubled, at times able to dismount and walk briskly alongside his donkey, keeping hold of the reins. Poor Jenny and her master parted company that same day, as a ballad recorded,

He sold his darling Jenny,
And a pony bought.

"Rabbi" Stainesby ran his last foot race in 1865 and, at forty, was the eldest of a field of five. He came third to win a small cash prize, but far more poignant was the realisation that his athletic days were over, his natural gift had all been spent.

There were those who remembered kindly his finest hours. He was spotted at one athletics meeting without a copper to his name and spectators with long memories collected among themselves and the old runner left that day with money in his pocket, just as in the old times. "Rabbi" must have carved quite a wide reputation for himself in his prime. He arrived in London with only seven pence in his pocket for the second Great Exhibition, in 1862. Those who knew him saw to it that he enjoyed the day and when it was time to head north for home he did so with a ten shillings advantage.

19

Those Curious Ley Lines

Some years ago, with a few friends, I visited Derbyshire's most famous prehistoric monument. Arbor Low, a great stone circle near Monyash, contains over forty recumbent stones within a foss or ditch which in turn is encompassed by an earthen rampart. Entrance is gained by causeways let in at the northern and southern ends. While nowhere near as spectacular as the Stonehenge or Avebury circles the monument is still impressive enough to be deservedly known as the "Stonehenge of the North." The area around is redolent of once being a most important place in the lives of the builders, the Bronze Age people, around four thousand years ago give or take a century or two.

One argument that surrounds the stones is whether or not they were originally upright or lie flat by design. Archaeological debate over the years has swung one or the other with the "Up" faction generally losing out to the "Down" party. A lesser mystery is the name "Arbor." For most it means to do with trees, of which not too many are to be seen on a bleak moorland upland. That spelling in that meaning is accepted as American; "arbour" being the standard English version. However "arbor" (in English) has a far older meaning: "axle or spindle on which thing revolves."* From the air, Arbor Low

---

* *OED*

does indeed have the appearance of a rough horizontal wheel (as would most stone circles), an observation that has given seekers of the mystical countless happy hours. And ignore claims that the circle was a clock-cum-calendar which foretold the seasons for an agricultural people. No farmer needs any calendar to tell him when to plough, sow, reap and mow. Even if he did it is highly unlikely he would enlist friends to help drag a few hundred tons of stones around into a circle and dig out enormous earthen banks to obtain this information. Anyway, two upright stones a few yards apart or, easier still, two wooden posts similarly distanced would be quite sufficient.

As we walked around the site we could not help but notice a large group of sombrely clothed people – the women in kaftans of forgettable hue and bearded men in various deployments of Army surplus clothing – all squatting in a circle. A circle within a circle. From their attitude they were engaged in serious business; sometimes holding hands, at other times pacing about with what I think were dowsing twigs. None of them was of a happy mien but they were most certainly intent on their strange ritual which clearly demanded deep concentration.

Eventually the human circle broke up, without any enhancement of expression, and we took the chance to question their activities. There is nothing quite so fanatical as a fanatic. Our questions were not fobbed off; indeed these drab-suited people were only too ready to answer. Perhaps they sensed apprentices to their curious quest, their search for the arcane factor. What they were doing, they patiently explained, was to locate and plot invisible and perfectly straight lines of strange powers that Arbor Low straddled, along with many other stone circles. Apparently the earth is criss-crossed with these unseen power lines, called ley lines for ease of reference. What precise power or energy they possessed was a total mystery. We gathered some people experienced a form of electric shock when they touched particular stones in the circles. There were a chosen few with such empathy for this "power" that they were routinely flung back quite sharply when they caressed them. Stonehenge sitting at a junction of dozens of ley lines is something of a high-powered generating station for this weird power. Arbor Low is ranked highly in the "grid" system, hence the group's activities that afternoon.

Arbor Low Stone Circle

One of my companions, more economical than most, queried that if he found one of these power lines could he plug into it and so obtain free and unlimited heating and lighting for his home? Such shallow frivolity swiftly terminated the conversation. Clearly we were lacking the necessary intellect to grasp what a wonderful thing was being pursued: one of the great mysteries coming right down from times before Man started to record his history.

For myself I was sufficiently intrigued to pursue the matter further and delve into ley lines. The theory claims that many of the prehistoric and some not quite so ancient sites throughout the British Isles are, if you draw linking lines on a reasonably large-scale map, standing on absolutely straight but invisible lines. This cannot happen by chance. Throw a handful of coins on the ground and notice how many will align in such a line. There is no point in just testing the theory with two coins in line, or even three. To get four or more in line you may have to throw many times. With seven or more the odds against contain many noughts. Getting into double figures, the odds become astronomical. So what do we think when six, seven or eight prehistoric sites, or ten or twelve, all lie on a perfectly straight but invisible ley line? More to the point, why should they?

To explain the theory in full takes too much time; with the occasional exception of a prominent rock formation (Robin Hood's Stride near Elton, for example) accept that the sites, such as ancient burial mounds, standing stones, hill forts, are all prehistoric. Nine Ladies stone circle on Stanton Moor is a significant site. Where churches are used as points of contact they are usually old in themselves and standing on sites of possible pagan origin. Some ley lines contain sites running into double figures; a surprising number stretch many miles. Arbor Low, depending on your degree of conversion to the theory, is an extraordinary junction. A few adherents claim over a hundred lines bisect the circle before hurrying on to other ancient sites with which Derbyshire is well-endowed.

There are societies devoted to seeking an explanation for the leys; some of the truly daft see them as guide lines for UFOs; others are quite happy with the unseen power theory. Occasionally they publish news letters; I once subscribed to one but since it proved well-nigh inexplicable with its arguments, coupled with a disconcerting ability on the part of members to see ley lines everywhere and anywhere, I soon dropped out. I did learn, however, that the ancient Chinese knew of these power lines and, being Chinese, decided not to build on them. Surely a difficult thing to prove?

As with that group at Arbor Low the pursuit of ley lines has become something akin to the search for the Holy Grail. One might declare that there is nothing in the theory at all, but does so in the face of considerable evidence. Strip away all the ideas as to what the lines are for, the power they are said to possess. The inquirer is left with the lines. And is there not some spiritual solace in being faced with a mystery with an answer that must surely dwell in the supernatural?

The story of ley line began in 1925 when Hereford-born Alfred Watkins published a book, *The Old Straight Track*. Well documented and amply illustrated, the product of many years' observation, it became a modest best-seller. Scorn was poured on it by the archaeological world, then even more notorious for its non-acceptance of outside thought. But anyone who reads the book must admit Watkins presented his case well. Moreover, the reader can follow his examples and detection methods with ease and then, lightly armed with map, compass, ruler and pencil, stride off into the countryside and find leys for himself.

Watkins is worth reading, but beware of those who followed. Many have refused to accept his conclusion of prehistoric tracks and sought less-mundane reasons. Some are quite extraordinary. Their findings in word and print are often incomprehensible, well-hidden behind a cascade of words more difficult to divine than locating ley lines in countryside where prehistoric sites are rare or difficult to recognise traces of.

In Derbyshire the searcher is well-catered for. Arbor Low apart there are plenty of prehistoric burial mounds or barrows, marked "lows" on any reasonable large-scale map. There are smaller stone circles. The Nine Stones circle on Harthill Moor and quite close to Robin Hood's Stride, well repays the diligent detective. A relatively unexplored area that should produce more of these invisible lines lies between Repton in the south of the county and eastwards towards Aston-on-Trent. Little evidence of prehistoric habitation is easily seen for the coming and going of different civilisations moving along the Trent valley has destroyed much of it. However, painstaking work by archaeologists and modern methods have located a cursus, several barrows and other indications that the area once was one of considerable importance.

20

"The Sailors' Friend"

Plimsoll, *Samuel 1824-1898. English social reformer, born in Bristol. He sat in Parliament as a Radical 1868-80, and through his efforts the Merchant Shipping Act was passed in 1876, providing for Board of Trade inspection of ships, and the compulsory painting of a* ***Plimsoll Line*** *to indicate safe loading limits.*

Thus, a standard entry in a dictionary of famous people. Not mentioned is that Plimsoll was a Member of Parliament for Derby. An acceptable definition of a social reformer is one who fights to improve the lot of those whose very lives, not to mention living and working standards, are subjugated to the demands of commerce, property and profit. A contemporary described Samuel Plimsoll's principle characteristic as that of "simplicity." He added that, had the reformer been less so, had counted the cost of what he was setting about, then he "would have shrunk from such a combat."

> "But he has begun the fight, and he will not shrink; for in these simple, artless, unsophisticated men there is often wonderful courage and perseverance."

Derby has not treated well the memory of this most humane of men. A comprehensive history of the city does not even afford him ten lines and those tell not of his mark on history but that he was not popular locally. There are no memorials, no statue in his honour. A contemporary satirical magazine

The Derby Ram attacked him viciously. A few years ago a member of the Derby public suggested a memorial window to the MP might be appropriate in the town hall. The council's leisure committee thought the Industrial Museum more fitting and, being politicians of the more general ilk, did nothing. Only Plimsoll Street in the north of Derby serves to recall this kindly, unsophisticated man. He had laid a foundation stone in 1880 in the wall of a chapel in Sacheveral Street, which later became the home for the Derby Little Theatre Club under the name of Derby Playhouse. The old building has been demolished and with it went the Plimsoll stone.

No. 26. THE DERBY RAM. *December* 11, 1868.

CABBY—"What! Want thrippence change out of a bob for drivin' of yer from the Station to the R'yal? *Then yer may summons me for it!*" (*Exit* Plimsoll, hoping no listeners were about).

Samuel Plimsoll entered this world on 10 February 1824 at the port of Bristol and grew up with a deep interest in the sea and those who sailed on it, particularly their welfare in a harsh and often brutal calling. His father, employed in the excise service, encouraged his son's interest.

At thirteen, Samuel's family moved to Sheffield and a small corner house in Regent Street in the Portobello district. He would remain for most of his life in the Yorkshire steel city. His developing energies and organising abilities came to the notice of the authorities and with it the appointment as secretary of the 1851 Great Exhibition at London's Crystal Palace. For a permanent living he had turned to the coal trade, finding Sheffield an excellent centre for a business which eventually made him a wealthy man. Marriage to Elizabeth Ann Railton in 1857 did nothing to hinder his career, she being the step-daughter of a rich and influential mine owner and iron founder.

Plimsoll did not come up with the idea of load-lines as a measure to prevent overloading of ships. That distinction belongs to James Hall, a philanthropic shipowner from Tynemouth, and even he was not being entirely original. Such a simple concept had been around for centuries. Venetian traders, for example, painted on the side of their ships a hollow circle bisected by a horizontal line. Plimsoll achieved his international recognition by fighting a hard, remorseless campaign against considerable odds to make such markings a legal requirement for merchant shipping. With success it became inevitable that they became known world-wide as the Plimsoll Line.

The urgent need for such an obvious safety measure became painfully apparent to him as a coal trader. Coastal vessels employed as colliers to work between the North East of England and the Thames were notorious for their unseaworthiness and owners who insisted on their being dangerously overloaded. Insurance cover would be negotiated, with the underwriters spreading the risk so thinly as to make payment disputes hardly worth the effort. Owners were doubly secured. If the cargo got through, they made a profit; if the collier sunk then the insurance pay-out would be pocketed. Safety of the crews was of little consequence in too many owners' thinking. According to Plimsoll, if sailors objected to going out to sea in a vessel loaded to within two feet of the water amidships, "they may be overawed by a policeman or committed to prison by a magistrate."

Statistics compiled through the 1860s and 1870s underlined the necessity for legislation. Over half the lives lost around British coasts were from sunken colliers. Plimsoll quoted an imaginary, but certainly average case, of a totally unsuitable ship being put to sea by an unscrupulous owner. An old ship, say of two hundred and fifty tons, would be put up for sale for breaking up. She was quite unfit for sea without more money being spent on her; even then she would have been worth more before the necessary repairs had been carried out. The purchaser would pay £50 and much to the previous owner's horror, and despite attempts to stop it, the vessel would be prepared for sea. Too rotten for caulking the ship would be painted over to conceal its sorry state.

To crew this death-trap, men were hired from distant ports since they would be ignorant of its background. To further disguise the old ship its name would be changed, an act which enraged Plimsoll. Then, with a cargo secured and insurance arranged, the "coffin ship" set sail. Whether or not it reached its destination would be of little monetary consequence to the owners; they collected either way.

Plimsoll set about his self-appointed battle for maritime reform and saw Parliament as the only arena. He first contested a Derby seat as a Liberal in 1865 but unsuccessfully. He had to run the gauntlet of tremendous opposition from newspapers and commercial interests, and suffered constant lampooning in *The Derby Ram.* Three years later came another election and this time he won through, taking the second seat for his party with more than two thousand votes.

An energetic man with a fondness for hyperbole and the dramatic gesture, Plimsoll's first attempt at Westminster to achieve his goal was to have been through a Private Member's Bill in 1871, but he had second thoughts.

Two years later he broadened his campaign by publishing a small book, *Our Seamen*, in which he set out his case for a shipping load-line. A somewhat extravagant work steeped in the foul machinations of ship owners and horrifying loss of life, Plimsoll footed the bill for its free distribution. He wanted as many as possible to understand precisely what he was about. Its publication created a sensation. The author had been meticulous over its presentation and newspapers noted his "curious plan" of introducing photographs of printed matter annotated and initialled by himself, underlining that documentary evidence had been carefully scrutinised. One newspaper described the book as "more than an indictment than appeal, and an indictment against the greatest of maritime peoples, of careless indifference to the lives of our sailors."

At the beginning of 1873 Samuel Plimsoll addressed his constituents at the Temperance Hall in Curzon Street. According to one report, "he was moved to tears" while reading out aloud extracts from the forthcoming *Our Seamen*. The audience was assured by their MP that should he fail during the next parliamentary session to have a Royal Commission set up, then he proposed to undertake a nation-wide tour to put his case fully before the people so that "the working men of the country would lift up their voices and say that this state of things should cease to exist." Plimsoll asked his constituents to free him, if necessary, of his obligations to attend the coming parliamentary session so that he could undertake such a tour. Put to the vote, approval was unanimously given.

There was a Royal Commission, and another Private Bill (rejected by three). *Our Seamen* had done its work well. In the end the Government decided to step in and a Merchant Shipping Bill came before the House and precipitated one of the most amazing outbursts ever during a Commons debate. Prime Minister Disraeli proposed postponing the Bill, which would incur a further year's delay. Overwrought and worn out from his exertions, Plimsoll jumped to his feet, arms flailing like windmills. In a volcano of anger he lay all about him. Wild statements abused the astonished ears of the House. He would not be thwarted at the final hurdle. Ship-owners were denounced in no uncertain terms; some, he shouted out, were of "murderous tendencies"; others "ship-knackers" and "maritime murderers." That some MPs were owners – "the greatest sinners in the trade" – served only to add fuel to the general uproar. Order was restored only after Plimsoll had been escorted out, still protesting and gesticulating. Derbyshire's Marquis of Hartington successfully proposed an adjournment of the discussion.

Samuel Plimsoll had won. His explosive outburst aroused even more public sympathy and newspaper support than *Our Seamen*. A week later, another Bill was laid before Parliament and received due approval; in 1876 the Plimsoll Line became law and a fact.

Not generally known is that Derby's MP was also responsible for another, somewhat lesser Bill, that of making railway companies provide footways in second and third class carriages. First class carriages already had them. All his life he had fought for better conditions for working men. In earlier years he had published pamphlets on the need for other reforms in the shipping industry. Nor had he overlooked the needs of those who earned their living on the canals. But the Merchant Shipping Bill had been his prime objective and with its success the "Sailors' Friend" decided his parliamentary career had served its purpose. At the 1880 election he resigned his seat in favour of Sir William Harcourt. Incoming and outgoing Members of Parliament for Derby were accorded a resounding public acclamation on the balcony of Derby's Midland Hotel.

Although he had quit public life Samuel Plimsoll's compassion for his fellow men remained unabated and 1890 found him elected the first president of the National Amalgamated Sailors' and Firemen's Union. Maritime affairs still commanded his attention and he campaigned vigorously against the abominable conditions under which cattle were transported.

Samuel Plimsoll died on 3 June 1898. Plagued in his later years by poor health, particularly diabetes, he retired to Folkestone. His death there was mourned by countless sailors as one who made their dangerous trade a little safer and ship-owners more responsible. His enduring memorial can be seen the world over, those series of load-lines painted on the side of every sea-going vessel. Or should be.

21

"I met the finest ram, Sir"

As I was going to Derby,
All on a market day,
I met the finest ram, Sir,
That was ever fed on hay.

So runs the opening verse of *The Derby Ram*, a ballad telling of a beast of gargantuan proportions. Outrageously enormous and wildly at variance with that bronze statue known as the Derby Ram in the city's Main Centre shopping precinct. A young lad sits astride the normal-sized creature holding on by a gold collar and, according to its sculptor, William Dudeney, symbolising the youth of Derby. It was unveiled in July 1963.

A rumbustious composition of many verses it is not heard all that often, which is a pity. The animal gave Derby County football club its nickname and the former Sherwood Foresters, Derbyshire's own regiment, always had a magnificent example of the breed as its official mascot. That regiment was the descendant of the old 95th Regiment of Foot which acquired the first of a long line of such mascots when serving in India during the time of the Indian Mutiny (1857-9). According to one story they came by the ram as a gift from a local ruler in recognition of the soldiers' good behaviour while stationed locally. Another version tells how the soldiers rescued a ram which unfortunately had tumbled down a well. And a ram is still doing service as regimental mascot, nowadays, following amalgamations, with the Worcestershire and Sherwood Foresters Regiment.

The wool upon his back, Sir
It drag'd upon the ground,
It was sold in Derby town, Sir
For forty thousand pounds.

Who wrote the ballad and when is a total mystery. And apart from a pallid possible derivative from Scotland, *The Ram of Diram*, remains unique to Derby. Much research has gone into trying to discover its origins but with singular lack of success. Most findings were published in the latter half of the last century, usually with the comment that local spoken lore dated the song about a century before. But there is no documentary back-up.

Any notion that it may have followed the old 95th Regiment acquiring a ram as a mascot are easily scotched for the earliest account of the ballad being sung rests in the 18th century and, of all places, in Connecticut. No less a person than George Washington, first president of the United States, is reported as having once taken a friend's twin boys on each knee and delighting them with the first four verses of *The Derby Ram*. Since Washington was of direct English descent it follows he must have picked it up from some member or friend of his family.

The butcher that killed the ram, Sir
Was drowned in the blood
The boy that held the pail, Sir,
Was carried away on the flood.

However, there is no reason to reject that the song may be far, far older. Possibly with roots in medieval times or even earlier. After all, the ram is one of the four great phallic symbols of ancient times, the others being the goat, the stag and the bull. And all were considered propitious for ritual sacrifice.

The ram held a particular place in people's estimation and ritual. In the 14th-century it served as the common prize for winners of wrestling matches. During May, a month steeped in folklore, the people of Holme on Dartmoor held a Ram Feast with the villagers running down a ram and then, complete with fleece, roasting him close by a granite pillar. Those fortunate to grab a slice of the meat were assured of good luck. Still in the West Country, each Whit Monday at Kingsteignton, Devon, a decorated carcase is paraded through the town and later roasted. Such ceremonies must have origins stretching back over the years and quite possibly into pagan times.

The Derby Ram

And, as at least one researcher noticed, there is a Ram (Aries) in the Zodiac. In a remarkable example of shaping facts to fit a theory it has been claimed that the verse which tells of the Derby Ram's tail being so long that it *"stretched right over to Ireland, Sir, And rang Saint Patrick's bell."* is surely evidence that the ram formed part of some long-forgotten religious cult in which blood sacrifices played a part.

The little boys of Derby
They came to beg his eyes,
To kick about the streets, Sir,
For they were football size.

An only slightly more acceptable claim as to antiquity can be found in Sidney Addy's *Household Tales* (1895). He linked the ballad with another called *The Old Tup* (a tup is a male sheep), which he recalled being sung in his childhood by young men, one of whom would be down on all fours and draped in a sheep's skin and horns. With the ending of the music, tup was "slain." Addy went on to connect the song with the Old Norse sagas contained in two literary collections known as the Edda in which some unidentified being of enormous proportions is slaughtered in a regular blood-bath.

Most would regard the connection as tenuous. But it is worth recalling that Derby's origins lie in the Viking settlement of Northworthy, built by a people well-versed in the Scandinavian sagas. Since no one has the slightest idea where Derby's stupendous beast emanated from then Addy's theory might as well be considered. It at least possesses the merit of imagination and whoever did compose *The Derby Ram* certainly did not lack in that sensibility.

Indeed, Sir, it's the truth, Sir,
For I was never taught to lie,
And if you go to Derby, Sir,
You may eat a bit of the pie

22

Lock-out

Not that long ago in a letter to a newspaper a local historian made the comment, "thus the stigma of (Derby) having been the flash point of England's first major trades union dispute . . . " Such a statement sits oddly with a member of a delicate profession which, if it is to remain true to itself, must practise detachment. The remark did not go unchallenged. In reply, a prominent trades union official made the obvious point that anti-trades union prejudices had been paraded. Moving along with such words as "snide," "contemptible," and "ridiculous," the official wrote of improvements brought about by his movement. He claimed that if "people to-day believe that these major achievements were the gift of philanthropic managements," then the historian had a much bigger task on his hands than lecturing to the trades union movement. A good beginning for a first-class row but, by design or lack of interest, the correspondence went no further.

Behind that brief exchange of letters lay the famous Derby silk trades lock-out of 1833-34 when workers in that prominent industry, members of the nascent trades union movement, gave warning of what power they might one day wield. In effect the dispute was a trial of strength between two forms of union, on one side the workers and on the other, factory owners and management.

What stirred the historian into action had been a newspaper article which stated that the 1833 lock-out was based at

Derby's historic silk mill on the banks of the River Derwent, the first in England. To-day it survives in the form of the city's comprehensive industrial museum. That the dispute started there is a popular misconception (as the historian quite properly pointed out) unwittingly aided by a nearby public house, the Old Silk Mill, which bears on a gable end a huge mural painted in 1986 which, under the title "Silk Mill Lock Out 1834," depicts scenes of the confrontation. The building stands on the site of a former Old Silk Mill pub, itself a converted mill worker's cottage demolished in 1924. There is no hard evidence that the mill had even been involved in the strike.

Further muddying the issue is the placing of a commemorative plaque alongside the silk mill's original gateway, a superb example from Derbyshire's iron master Robert Bakewell.

Background to the lock-out was the demand by silk workers for the right to form a trades union in order to negotiate better pay and working conditions. Both were areas in which improvements were sorely needed, a fact reflected in the appalling conditions workers were obliged to live out their lives under virtual domination by mill owners.

Haunted by the French Revolution and the spectre of revolt among the working classes the Government had passed a law in 1800 forbidding trade unions. Twenty-four years later reformers achieved their goal when the Government passed the Combination Acts permitting workers to combine under such headings as wages, hours and working conditions. The Acts were sternly against any form of intimidation, obstruction or coercion on the part of the workers; and, *quid pro quo*, by employers.

Following upon the Acts came an army of too many, too small, unions, but by 1833 common sense and amalgamation had prevailed with most workers members of the Grand National Consolidated Trade Union. And in that year Derby's silk mill lock-out took place.

Rykneld Mill, Derby

Clearly the town's mill owners were agitated by the workers combining. While superficially acknowledging their employees right to do just that, the owners decided to fight them on the grounds they had been obliged to swear a secret oath which they interpreted as being either coercive or intimidatory.

In late November Mr Frost, of the Peet and Frost silk mill in Bridge Street, (to-day the Rykneld Mill) fired one of his workmen who declined to be fined for faulty work. If the work was in fact faulty may be doubted; more likely the move was to force the issue of trade unionism in the silk industry and drive it from Derby's mills. Mr Frost's action precipitated an immediate mass walk-out by the discharged man and his fellow workers. Bridge Street fell silent, the looms stilled.

Before long eight hundred mill workers, men and women, were on strike, with every indication the number would rise. Worried employers met in the King's Head Hotel Inn in the Cornmarket on 23 November to discuss what action should be taken. That their solution, the Declaration of Twenty (the number of employers signing), could not be seen as anything else but coercive or intimidatory, both illegal under the Acts, did not seem to occur to anyone. Moreover the Declaration asserted that each signatory would cease to employ any trade union member, nor take back into employment anyone who was a member. Employers agreed they held "deliberate conviction that a prompt and vigorous and persevering resistance to the Trade Union is absolutely necessary to protect the joint interests of the master, to preserve the commerce of the Country, and to secure the true interests of the workers themselves." That last point could only be described as undiluted hypocrisy and arrogant condescension made against a backdrop of appallingly long hours, poor pay, poor conditions and, in some cases, payment by tokens redeemable only in shops established by employers.

Mill owners distributed what they purported to be a copy of the secret oath sworn by trade union members. If the document was genuine, and there are doubts, then it bore, as some newspapers noted, a strong resemblance to the oaths taken by members of the Freemasons and Oddfellows societies, strongholds of employers. Secret oaths were proscribed by law.

A few days into December and one thousand three hundred were out on strike, a number swelled by workers from other industries, building, weaving and pottery. Special constables, backed up by a detachment of the 2nd Dragoon Guards, were enrolled to protect property and maintain law and order. While the authorities quite naturally would have been concerned over the possibility of riots (the violent Reform Riots two years earlier remained fresh in people's minds) the lock-out overall was comparatively peaceful.

There were some scuffles between strikers and "black-legs," workers brought in from other towns. One man found himself being transported to Australia following a stabbing incident in Brook Street close by the gates of Peet and Frost's mill. More common were the three-month prison sentences imposed by magistrates. Other official action, according to a visiting trade union official, included the denying of parish relief to a widow subsisting on potato peelings because her son "smelt" of trade unionism. Another widow and her daughters who had been dismissed because they "smelt" similarly, were discovered locked in their house and in bed because there was no food.

The Church did not like what was going on. Derby-born Thomas Gisborne, Prebendary of Durham, in a long letter to the Press exhorted the strikers to return to their looms. He claimed that he had grown up among the workers of Derby, the sort of statement that prompts inquiry as to actual proximity. Pointing out that taking of the oath was contrary to Holy Scripture, he warned of the awful consequences of disregarding the Divine Word.

As already stated the lock-out overall was well-conducted. This was illustrated by the responsible decision by strike leaders to move their followers out of Derby and up to Duffield for the period of the Shrove Tuesday and Ash Wednesday football matches, an ancient form of mayhem now banned in Derby but still played every Shrove Tuesday at Ashbourne. Since the games were violent confrontations and generally caused unrest, the strikers thought discretion the prudent card to play. So off they went to Duffield, a long, flag-led column headed by bands and six hundred women. Behind came some fourteen hundred men. Somewhere among them all trundled the provision carts. At Duffield they were joined by fellow unionists from Belper, Heage and Swanwick.

Considering the odds stacked against them, the workers were remarkable in holding out for five months. Union pay funds dried up early in the turn-out and ambitious plans to buy machinery and trade on their own account were doomed from the start. Inevitably the historic action stumbled, fell and finally died on 21 April 1834. Workers trickled back to the mills and slowly the looms of Derby's principal industry began to hum again. For six hundred workers there was no return to work. Not necessarily the doing of vengeful employers, but because new workers were already in place and there were too few entries on the mills' order books.

23

Man's Best Friend

But thinks, admitted to that equal sky,
His faithful dog shall bear him company.

Occasionally, the collie dog would leave the old man's body and scavenge for food. Despite wind, frost and snow some could always be found. At least for a dog wise in the ways of the wild moor. Dead sheep, birds and rabbits, all victims of the numbing cold of a moorland winter. Having eaten, Tip, for that was her name, would lurch back to the corpse and once again resume her unquestioned vigil. Round and round she loped, padding a path through the coarse, cutting heather. As days passed into weeks and the weeks into months the walk became a stagger, sometimes barely a crawl. There were times when she lay down, exhausted by her labours. Bleak, cruel, biting Nature would try to drive Tip away from her life's task, companion to an old man. Frost, snow and the eternal icy wind attacked, withdrew and attacked again and again. Then one day a farmer's helper, Sam Bingham, seeking scattered sheep on Ronksley Moor, found the faithful Tip, emaciated, wet and weak, lying a few yards from her dead master. The pair were four miles from the nearest inhabited house. The date was 27 March, 1954; for over three terrible months Tip had kept her watch. As her master's pitiful remains were brought down to the valley the collie's remarkable story became known to the world.

The vast, inhospitable moors dominating the northern

reaches of Derbyshire have claimed many lives. Once one has climbed out of the steep-sloped valleys which pierce their nether regions, the moors are seen to be rather gently undulating, flat almost in parts. Miniature treacherous gullies known as groughs cut into the heather land allowing water to flow away down to the valleys. Nothing much grows there except heather, glorious once a year in its purple, and other hardy growth where the unceasing winds cannot probe and scour. Treacherous land, too. Many an aeroplane has crashed on the two wildernesses known as Bleaklow and Kinder Scout. Most of the sites are known, plotted and recorded by a society dedicated to that task. Remains are there to be seen. One wonders what the survivors of those crashes must have felt when they struggled out of their near-tombs of twisted metal and gazed on a land without feature or mercy.

Summer is the recommended time to walk these wastelands. And many do for there is an awesome fascination, a compulsion almost. Life is there, too.

Rabbits make a break for it. Skylarks rise and rise to pour out their melody and make us believe in God. Partridge and grouse rise at the sound of human approach. But their flight is low and swift, just skimming the round in obedience to some arcane instinct instilled by death-dealing shotguns.

Tip's master was eighty-six years old Joseph Tagg, a retired shepherd of national repute. He had been born at Ronksley Farm, last house in the Derwent Valley and demolished around 1910 with the coming of the Howden Reservoir. All his life he had walked and worked over the surrounding unforgiving moors, tending sheep and training top-class collie dogs to keep the flocks under control. For a great many years Mr Tagg had worked as a shepherd for the Duke of Rutland before deciding to venture out on his own account. For he had a way with dogs and in the 1920s his reputation was such that a buyer from the United States was quite happy to hand over £1,000 for a collie trained by the Derbyshire shepherd. By any standards it was a huge sum but then the buyer wanted the best.

If anyone knew those moorlands, Joseph Tagg did. There was not a declivity, not a grough nor the remotest corner of Bleaklow mountain he had not traversed at some time in his long life. When, with the faithful Tip padding by his side, he set off on 12 December, 1953, it was probably nothing more than a ramble through long-familiar territory. He headed up the Derwent Valley and was last seen making for Slippery Stones. From that isolated spot he must have turned and headed back down the valley but, instead of making for Marebottom, Joseph Tagg turned his footsteps west into the rising valley of the River Westend, a waterway born high up Bleaklow Hill. When he failed to return to his niece's home where he spent his retirement years, the reaction was swift. Ramblers, shepherds, farmers, police and a unit from the nearby Royal Air Force Mountain Rescue Service combed the moors. Eventually the army of helpers ran into hundreds. No trace of either master nor his dog was ever found until far too late.

How often didst thou think his silence was
slumber
When the wind waved his garments, how oft didst
Thou start?

By even Bleaklow standards the winter of 1953 was a hard one. But over the fifteen weeks before Tip and her dead master were found the search was never abandoned. Ironically, one search party rested for a quick lunch break within two hundred yards from where Joseph Tagg's remains lay crumpled within the circle padded out by Tip.

They carried the faithful collie down to the valley and a few days later Mr Tagg was buried. Tip's ordeal touched a common chord and within a few days she had become something of a celebrity. School children living around Dartmoor, another harsh moorland fastness, saved their pennies and

Tip's memorial

bought a special collar. The National Canine Defence League awarded their Bronze Medal. A granite memorial stone paid for by contributions from all over the world was erected on the western bank of Derwent Dam, close to the majestic wall which divides that dam from the Ladybower Reservoir and a familiar sight to ramblers and sightseers. Tip was not at the unveiling. She had died a few weeks earlier, in February 1955. She never really recovered from the terrible ordeal suffered for all those weeks on the high ground overlooking the simple memorial.

Tip herself was not buried by the memorial but close to the spot where she had guarded her beloved master, above where the River Westend tumbles down from Bleaklow Hill. Only for food did she ever leave him. For Tip and her breed there is no other way.

24

Conspiracy?

The voice assured me, "Actually, you can't miss it." I had telephoned the City Council's Cemeteries office, ironically listed under Leisure Services Department, to enquire the whereabouts of a grave. My informant told me to look in the older part of Derby's vast two-part cemetery up Nottingham Road, enter by the somewhat imposing main gate and turn right. A few more directions and then ultimate proof that I had the right grave. "The headstone's fallen flat on its face," the official explained. Nothing could be read of the inscription, of course, but there could be no doubt it was the correct place for no other neighbouring headstones were similarly inclined.

This tale is of a travesty of justice. It is also a tale of conspiracy. And as the bizarre details unfolded at London's Old Bailey in the early days of March, 1917, they made international news headlines. Famous names appeared in court. Sir Frederick Smith ["F.E." in legal circles], Attorney General, who had prosecuted the troublesome Sir Roger Casement the previous year, and possessor of one of the sharpest legal minds of the day. Bernard Spilsbury, most famous of pathologists, who presented such telling evidence against Crippen and also George Joseph Smith at the notorious "Brides in the Bath" trial. And when the conspirators had been disposed of there arrived on the scene Mrs Emmeline Pankhurst, leader of the militant movement for women's suffrage. David Lloyd George, Britain's Prime Minister of a few months, did not put in an appearance, but since it was his planned assassination that brought everyone else together his name could properly be added to the list.

After the sentences had been handed down by Mr. Justice Low general agreement followed that justice had been done. A nest of foul-mouthed, would-be killers put away where they could do no harm. However, in the years following there were many who came to question if there ever had been a conspiracy to slay the Prime Minister. Which in turn could suggest that one had been laid against the Wheeldon family.

The plot to assassinate the Prime Minister, and Lloyd George would have been the second to suffer such a fate, was hatched at 12 Pear Tree Road, Derby. Then as now it was fronted by a small shop where, in 1916, Alice Wheeldon, the leading conspirator, traded in second-hand clothes.

Mrs Wheeldon was a suffragette, pacifist, atheist and socialist; nowadays some would add feminist. The unceasing, mindless slaughter of tens of thousands of British soldiers as the Great War of 1914-18 raged over Belgium and France so distressed her that she had taken to harbouring conscientious objectors on the run. Her house in Pear Tree Road became a staging post in an underground system for smuggling them out of harm's way. In this she and her family could hardly have been unique; there must have been others around the country.

A striking woman of fifty, Alice Wheeldon was aided by her two attractive daughters. Hetty, a scripture teacher despite a professed atheism, still lived with her; Winifred, married to Alfred Mason a college laboratory assistant who wore his hair longer than the fashion, lived in Southampton. This then was the quartet which would end up at the Old Bailey charged with plotting Lloyd George's death.

The backdrop to the Wheeldons' story is important. By 1916 the Great War had staggered into its bloodiest passage.

Alice Wheeldon's grave

Summer saw the battlefield of the Somme drenched in blood and heard the agonised screams of the wounded and demented. Twenty thousand soldiers lost their lives in the opening assault alone. In some English towns there were streets wherein not a single house remained untouched by the awesome butchery as fathers, sons and lovers died in despairing efforts to gain the presumed advantage of a few blood-soaked yards.

The Wheeldons and the Masons, sheltering those choosing to avoid the killing fields, were certainly not alone in their criticism of the Government, in castigating Lloyd George, perhaps even wishing aloud for his death, however futile that event would prove. That they were brought to trial could suggest the authorities were looking for a morale-booster or maybe a stern warning to others similarly minded. Looking at the flimsy evidence the notion is not too far-fetched. In 1916 Parliament passed the Military Service Act, a move followed by the arrest of no less than six thousand objectors. Some were shipped over to France, made to stand trial before a court-martial and be sentenced to No. 1 Field Punishment, a brutality known among the troops as "the crucifixion."

In December 1916 the quartet were arrested by police at Pear Tree Road [the Masons were frequent visitors] and charged with conspiring to murder the Prime Minister and Arthur Henderson, a member of the wartime Cabinet. The method was to be by poisoning. There is no disputing that poisons, strychnine and curare, were procured by Mason, posted to Derby and intercepted by the postal authorities. Mrs Wheeldon explained they were for use against guard dogs at detention centres confining conscientious objectors. Derby magistrates considered the Crown's evidence and then remanded all four for eventual trial at the Old Bailey. By to-day's standards the case most likely would have been thrown out at that stage for lack of more substantial evidence.

There lingered a taint about that evidence. The case for the prosecution rested almost entirely on two men employed by the Ministry of Munitions, but operating as secret service agents possibly *agents provocateur.* The senior agent was never called upon at the trial to give his testimony.

Appearing for the Crown prosecution team was a formidable battery of legal artillery headed by the Attorney General, "F.E." Smith, and backed up by two King's Counsel and a Junior as well as a dozen or so expert advisers. The Wheeldons were represented by a Mr Riza, said to be of Persian extraction and reputedly related to the Royal family of that country. By his side their barrister retained the sole support of one solicitor. This one-sided line-up occasioned one newspaper to adopt a condescending attitude, remarking on Riza's lone stance as exciting such sporting sympathy "as Englishmen are bound to feel in a little chap who is fighting big ones."

Riza fought the good fight but was always out-gunned. Sir Frederick made great play of the bad language said to be used by the Wheeldons. In an age more polite than now foul speech was severely frowned upon and its reported prolific use might influence a jury's right-mindedness. One might wonder what bearing it had on the charge of conspiracy to murder other than creating prejudice. Alice Wheeldon, "F.E." stated, used "language of the most obscene and disgusting character." Her two daughters, the Attorney General thundered on, employed language "disgusting and obscene in the mouth of the lowest form of criminal." All three women he declared to the jury, were in "a diseased moral condition." But as to how the gang proposed to actually carry out the crime with which they were charged, the where and when, Sir Frederick astonishingly offered no evidence at all. His two King's Counsel and one Junior sitting alongside on their benches were similarly unforthcoming.

Both agents on whom the Crown's case rested had infiltrated the Wheeldon household on the pretext of seeking shelter. Alex Gordon was the leader and despite his deep involvement never gave evidence. His accomplice was Herbert

John Ward Booth, formerly a barrister's clerk and known as "Comrade Bert" to the Wheeldons.

Booth did give evidence and assured the jury that Alice Wheeldon told him £300 had been made available by the women's suffragette movement [not to her personally] for an attempt on Lloyd George's life. Booth had nothing more to add to the prosecution case; nor did he say how the accused proposed to get close enough to the Prime Minister and Henderson, never mind administer the poisons.

Bernard Spilsbury, the pathologist, made a brief appearance in the witness stand, described the properties of strychnine and curare and then departed.

Virtually the entire case against the Wheeldon family was built up behind the scenes by the shadowy Alex Gordon. For some years after the trial John S. Clarke, a friend of Alice Wheeldon and later a Glasgow MP, pursued a vendetta against the man but failed to produce anything tangible. Many more years were to pass before some little substance could be given to someone by then deceased.

Summing up for the defence Riza pointed out that many people used expressions such as "he ought to be shot," or "ought to be hanged," and cited Ulster where all sorts of threats were issued yet never materialised. About the mysterious Gordon, the barrister argued that the agent should have been produced and subjected to cross-examination in the interests of public safety. "If this method of prosecution goes unchallenged, it augurs ill for England," he warned the jury.

Cold thick fog, able courier for the raging 'flu epidemic, smothered the Old Bailey on 10 March as the Wheeldons filed into the dock for the last time. None displayed any emotion as the verdicts were delivered. Hetty was found not guilty, but difficult to see why. The remaining three were not so fortunate. Alice Wheeldon was sentenced to prison for ten years, daughter Winifred to five years and her husband Alfred to seven.

Before the court stood down Mrs Emmeline Pankhurst, leader of the suffragettes, received permission to address the assembly. She was anxious to refute any suggestion made by Booth in evidence that her movement, the Women's Political and Social Union, had ever offered money for an attempt on the life of Lloyd George. Indeed, the WPSU never countenanced the taking of human life. Curious that Mrs Pankhurst was not called upon to give this statement in evidence.

Nine months later, her health declining, Alice Wheeldon, Prisoner No. 889, was released from London's Holloway Prison, believed on the personal intervention of Lloyd George. She returned to Derby, not to her old home in Pear Tree Road, but to live out the remaining months of her life a virtual recluse in London Road at a house close by the present day Alvaston Park. She died on 20 February 1919, yet another 'flu victim. Hetty had predeceased her from the same cause. Winifred and Alfred Mason were freed within two years of sentencing. Later the couple separated, Winifred to run a dairy business in Southampton. Alfred disappeared from view.

Authority conspired that Alice Wheeldon's funeral would not be made the occasion for any public display. Dying at her second home, the body was smuggled out and spirited to a secret destination to await burial. The ploy proved quite successful, leaving a large crowd waiting vainly for the funeral cortege outside the house. Despite this precaution a second crowd did succeed in gathering at the burial and conducted an anti-Government demonstration.

Reporting the burial ceremonies the local newspaper used the odd phrase "sensational simplicity" when describing the trappings devoid as they were of any Christian ethos. As they lowered Alice Wheeldon's coffin into the ground her son, William, with an extravagant gesture, draped a red flag on its descending lid.

No name was recorded on her headstone. Instead there

appeared an inscription contradictory for someone professing no belief in Christianity. It read:

I will have mercy upon her
that had not obtained mercy

And so came to an end the strange story of the Pear Tree conspiracy, leaving some to ask the question: which group were the true conspirators – the Wheeldons or the Government? Over sixty years were to pass before a revealing light was shed on what was possibly Derby's greatest criminal case.

***

In the early Eighties came renewed interest in the Wheeldons and their conspiracy. A Derby theatre group produced a play and a feminist wrote a book.

Both efforts followed a remarkable BBC 2 television programme, *A Plot To Kill Lloyd George*, screened in 1983 after considerable research. Alice Wheeldon was played by the distinguished actress Brenda Bruce. The television verdict delivered confirmed what many had thought. The Wheeldons were undoubtedly innocent of the charges, their greatest "crime" probably that of being too vociferous in their condemnation of Lloyd George. When television investigators spoke with people who remembered the sensation they found several reluctant at first to speak.

And Alex Gordon finally stepped out, just a little, from the shadows. From Leicester, he was a former newspaper reporter inclined to mental instability. He, and presumably Booth, had been recruited by the Government intelligence agency MI5 to investigate possible threats of sabotage in Derby, home of the Rolls-Royce factory whose aero-engines were of such vital importance to the war effort. Gordon wheedled his way into the Wheeldons' home and, according to the investigation team, it was he who planted into the Wheeldons' thinking the notion they procure poisons as a means of "getting the boys out of internment camps."

Letters were written to the Masons in Southampton asking Alfred to send up the poisons. Only those letters not mentioning for what they were intended – the killing of guard dogs – were used in the building of the Crown's case. Those that did were put to one side. A point argued years before by those seeking justice for Alice Wheeldon after her release.

So great was the odium attached to Gordon's name after the Old Bailey trial that the authorities considered he best be removed from view and so they shipped him off to South Africa.

Should the curious go to visit Alice Wheeldon's grave they will find it easily enough among the long, stone ranks of upright headstones: flat on its face, the inscription hidden to view. In death, as at the Old Bailey all those years ago, not all is revealed.

25

Witches

Thou shalt not suffer a witch to live

(Exodus xii.18.)

An old tale tells that when two young sons of one of the Dukes of Rutland fell ill and died at Haddon Hall the attending doctors declared they simply did not understand why. In their learned opinion such ignorance meant that witchcraft must surely be the cause. Two sisters living nearby later confessed, presumably under pain of torture, to being witches and bringing about the deaths and were duly executed. The mother must have come under suspicion since she felt sufficiently moved to declare that if in any way she had been involved in the brothers' deaths, she hoped she too would die. No sooner were those fateful words spoken than she proved as good as her word!

How much credibility can be attributed to what is a fairly typical example of supposed witchcraft? Safe to assume is that the girls were horribly mutilated before blurting out their guilt. Also the doctors had employed a not unknown stratagem when professionally embarrassed and blamed others rather than their own medical shortcomings. The mother's abrupt demise may be someone's imagination improving an otherwise unexceptional story; that is if you choose not to believe in witchcraft.

Witches are an odd and ancient subject, rather like fairies.

We all accept they do not exist and yet, presuming some slight talent for drawing, we would all sketch quite similar pictures of them. That would be true in many countries, not just England. Why this should be so is another day's work. As is a study of witchcraft itself. To consult a few of the numerous books on the subject would only create further confusion and summon up more questions than are answered.

Derbyshire would have had its fair share of witches although examples are quite rare. Most famous, or infamous, is the case of the Bakewell witches which occurred in 1608.

An itinerant Scotsman, a pedlar by trade, had been lodging at the house of a Mrs Stafford in Bakewell and, unable or unwilling to settle his account, had been thrown out onto the street early one morning dressed only in his night attire. His clothes Mrs Stafford retained until he returned with the money owed her. The Scotsman suffered further humiliation shortly after when arrested by a constable of the watch and hauled up before the magistrates. Seeing an opportunity to take his revenge on Mrs Stafford and at the same time explain his own embarrassing situation, the pedlar told a remarkable story.

Asleep in his lodgings he had been awakened by a shaft of light coming up between a gap in the floorboards. Curious, for it was late, he arose and peeped down. In the room below Mrs Stafford and another woman, a friend, were busily preparing to go out. Ready, they chanted the following rhyme:

Over thick, over thin
Now, Devil, to the cellar in Lunnon (London)

To the watcher's amazement the two women promptly disappeared and their room plunged into darkness. Baffled, the Scotsman sat on his bed shivering in his night clothes. His puzzlement got the better of him and he repeated the lines. Amazement struck again and this time he himself abruptly disappeared from the house. A mighty wind plucked him up and whirled him higher and higher until he suddenly came down to earth. Or, to be more precise, in a cellar. For the third time that weird night he was amazed, this time by the sight of Mrs Stafford and her friend in another part of the cellar wrapping up silks and other items. Instinctively the pedlar knew the parcels contained stolen goods. Mrs Stafford spotted her lodger and she handed him a glass of wine which he drank gratefully. Quickly he fell into a deep sleep and when he awoke discovered that he was outside Mrs Stafford's Bakewell house, trembling in his night attire and being arrested by a constable on a charge of vagrancy.

Incredibly this blatantly mischievous tale was believed by the listening magistrates who, no doubt, were themselves amazed by the Scotsman's strange adventures. Nor were they in any doubt that what they heard was nothing less than evidence of witchcraft.

Mrs Stafford and her friend were arrested and despite vehement protests were put to death.

Another incident, not so well known but better documented, concerns the notorious Boy of Burton, Thomas Darling. When a lad of fourteen he became lost in Winsell (Winshill?) wood on 27 February, 1596. He solved his dilemma by wandering around until he stumbled across a familiar pathway which led back home. Once there, he suffered a series of fits. Under their influence he told his family an extraordinary tale of seeing a green cat and green angels. The story improved. Thomas had "witnessed" other weird sights: a man emerging from a chamber pot, the flames of hell and the heavens opening. A doctor was called in and he diagnosed worms. Unfortunately for Mother Alice Gooderidge of Stapenhill, an old, unprepossessing woman of sixty, the boy heard mention of witchcraft during the doctor's visit. There were more fits over the next few days. And then the Boy of Burton told another story.

While wandering about the wood he had come across a little old woman with three ugly warts disfiguring a wrinkled face. She was Mother Gooderidge and as she walked by Thomas broke wind, an impolite function which so enraged her that she cursed the boy and told him that while she would go to heaven he would go to hell. Officialdom approached Mother Alice. She agreed she had indeed met Thomas Darling, who, in addition to his lapse in social behaviour, called her "the witch of Stapenhill." In retort, she broke into rhyme:

Every boy doth call me witch,
But did I make thy arse to itch?

So this poor old crone, her life undoubtedly made more miserable by malicious fools such as the Burton Boy, was arrested. She suffered the most appalling indignities and torture at the hands of her inquisitors. They shaved her body to permit a closer search for physical evidence of a witch. An unfortunate inability to recite the Lord's Prayer was greeted as substantial incriminating evidence. More torture followed. Alice Gooderidge's feet were forced into a new pair of shoes and she was then violently held close to a roaring fire. The shoes grew exceedingly hot and in intense pain and obviously willing to say anything to put a stop to the agony, shrieked out she would reveal all.

Mother Gooderidge must have been a tough old lady for upon release "she confessed nothing." Later, however, she admitted to being helped by the Devil in the likeness of a dog. Oddly enough she was not sentenced to death but instead to Derby to serve a year's imprisonment. Thomas Darling later confessed he had faked the fits and "revelations", but too late to help Alice Gooderidge. She, poor woman, had died while languishing in Derby gaol.

Why were some females, usually old and bending beneath the years, thought of as witches and, consequently, so barbarously persecuted? Witches were nothing new as the opening Biblical quotation demonstrates. These women, often demented creatures who imagined strange things and made stranger claims, were feared, ostracised, humiliated but as a rule rarely went in fear of their lives. That held true for centuries. Then in the 13th-century there came a terrible change and with it a murderous pogrom against witches that survived well into the 17th-century. Ethnic cleansing is no new concept.

It would be impossible to say how many tens of thousands of poor, ill-served creatures all over Europe were accused of the vilest of abominations (frequently of a gross and debased sexual nature), suffered the most obscene torture and then sentenced to die horrible deaths. Such were the tortures, and such the nature of the charges, the suggestion is there that the accusers' minds were more warped than those of their hapless half-crazed victims. And how curious that none of the accused ever called upon the supernatural powers they were alleged to possess to free themselves from their frightful situations. No one, it seems, pondered that question; nor did anyone ask why had none of the accusers nor their mentors had ever witnessed any of the vile acts, nor seen the weird and dreadful creatures witches reputedly could summon up from the dank recesses of the Devil's kingdom.

Why this holocaust came about and plagued Europe for centuries can be laid at the feet of Pope Gregory IX, founder of the Inquisition in 1231. The Inquisition soon come up with witches here, there and everywhere. Some historians have put forward the theory that the Church's influence was waning and to re-assert previously unquestioned authority dreamed up demons, devils and witches to frighten people into turning to the Church for salvation. In 1486 came the publication of one of the most dreadful documents ever visited on mankind. *Malleus Maleficarum (The Witches' Hammer)* was written by two Dominican monks and prefaced by a Bull of Pope Innocent VIII. That same Pope also entertained a hearty and practised detestation of Jews.

Anyone reading *The Witches' Hammer* to-day would wonder how such ridiculous rubbish ever came to be believed. Were there no challenging intellects? It is nothing more than an hysterical diatribe against witches, describing their supernatural powers of evil, their diabolical behaviour and, even worse, how to recognise them, to torture them into confessions and laid down what form of deaths they should die. All produced without the slightest hint of evidence that any intelligent, or just plain sensible, mind might question. Of course, there were those who exploited *The Witches' Hammer* for their own ends.

England possessed in James I a king not only stupid but extremely superstitious. He wrote *Demonologie*, a book which turned out to be nothing more than an updating of *Malleus Maleficarum.* Ascending the throne in 1603 he passed an Act which laid down precisely what should happen to witches, which added little to what had been going in Britain and Europe for the past two or three hundred years. During his twenty-two year reign it has been estimated that over three thousand unfortunate women were condemned to death for practising witchcraft, among them, it should be noted, Mrs Stafford and her equally unfortunate friend at Bakewell.

The witch of legend

26

Nothing More to be Said

Manchester newspapers in the early days of November 1745 carried the following report from Chapel-en-le-Frith, dated 1 November:

> "If any credit be due to history, especially to the more antient ones, we find, times of publick calamity, & great revolutions, have frequently been preceded by prodigies, & uncommon appearance in nature; if what follows shall appear to be something of that kind, you may depend upon the Truth in every particular.
>
> In a Church* about three miles distant from us, the indecent custom still prevails, of burying the dead in the place set aside for the devotions of the living; but, as the parish is not exceeding populous, one would scarce imagine the inhabitants of the Grave should be straitened for want of room, yet so it should seem; for, on the last day of last August, several hundreds of bodies arose in the open day, out of the Grave there at once, to the great astonishment and terror of several spectators, of unquestioned veracity, from whose mouths I had the account.

---

* *The church has been identified as the chapel in Hayfield, north of Chapel-en-le-Frith, and in another version of this story the bodies are said to have arisen from a communal grave for flood victims.*

They arose, as I said, out of the Grave, and immediately ascended towards heaven, singing in concert as they mounted along. They had not any winding sheets about them, yet did not appear quite naked. Their vesture seemed to be streaked with gold, interlaced with sable, and skirted with white, but exceeding light, as was judged by the agility of their motion, and the swiftness of their ascent. They left a most fragrant and delicious odour behind them, but were quickly out of sight; and what is become of them since, plus in what distant region of this vast universe they have taken up as their abode, no mortal can tell.

We assure our readers, the above is literally true, and next week we shall publish such testimonies about it, as must convince everyone."